# JU LOVE

## R.T. KENDALL

# JUST
# LOVE

The Christian's radical answer to life's problems

## R. T. KENDALL

CHRISTIAN FOCUS

© R. T. Kendall
ISBN 1-85792-273-5
ISBN 978-1-85792-273-8

10 9 8 7 6 5 4 3 2 1

Published in 1997
Reprinted 2006
by
Christian Focus Publications Ltd.,
Geanies House, Fearn, Ross-shire
IV20 1TW, Scotland, Great Britain.
www.christianfocus.com

Cover design by Danie Van Straaten

Printed by Nørhaven Paperback A/S, Denmark

# Contents

Preface........................................................7

1. The Most Excellent Way ........................11

2. The Language of Love ..........................19

3. So Near and Yet So Far ........................27

4. Brokenness..........................................33

5. The Fruit of Brokenness........................45

6. Nothing to Prove ................................57

7. The Art of Forgetting (1)........................67

8. The Art of Forgetting (2)........................73

9. Forgiving Ourselves............................81

10. No Axe to Grind................................93

11. Letting God Be God............................103

12. Coping Under Pressure ......................111

13. The Power of Love............................119

14. Opting for Excellence ........................133

15. Perfect Love ....................................141

16. Growing Up ....................................151

17. When God Tells Us Why ....................163

18. Why Not the Best? ............................173

Appendix..............................................183

To
Abbie

# Preface

This book was written during my darkest hour. I cannot say when or what the circumstances were, only to let the readers know that in the darkest year of my life the book emerged. Deep suffering taught me to love more than ever, and all that I had previously taught and tried to experience in terms of total forgiveness has been enlarged upon and filled out by what I have discovered about 1 Corinthians 13. I sincerely pray that God will bless it to you, the reader, as I have been blessed.

I dedicate this book to my stepmother, Abbie, who has been an angel over the years. My own mother died when I was seventeen. My father remarried a year later. In his time of sorrow God gave him, in a rather extraordinary manner, a promise that he would meet and marry an Abigail! It was when the Lord gave him 1 Samuel 25. Imagine his amazement when, only a few months later, an old friend of his introduced him to Miss Abigail West of Fitzgerald, Georgia. My Dad now lives in a nursing home with Alzheimer's disease, and I just wish that he had the presence of mind to know that I'm dedicating this book to his beloved Abbie. I wish I could say that I always showed the love of 1 Corinthians 13 to her when she first came into our lives.

It is now that I can appreciate all that she went through and want in some way to show my gratitude to her by dedicating this book lovingly to her.

My warm thanks to Christian Focus, Malcolm Maclean in particular, and to Alison Linnell who worked hard in editing the material.

R. T. Kendall
July, 1997

And now I will show you the most excellent way. [1]If I speak in the tongues of men and of angels, but have not love, I am only a resounding gong or a clanging cymbal. [2]If I have the gift of prophecy and can fathom all mysteries and all knowledge, and if I have a faith that can move mountains, but have not love, I am nothing. [3]If I give all I possess to the poor and surrender my body to the flames, but have not love, I gain nothing.

[4]Love is patient, love is kind. It does not envy, it does not boast, it is not proud. [5]It is not rude, it is not self-seeking, it is not easily angered, it keeps no record of wrongs. [6]Love does not delight in evil but rejoices with the truth. [7]It always protects, always trusts, always hopes, always perseveres.

[8]Love never fails. But where there are prophecies, they will cease; where there are tongues, they will be stilled; where there is knowledge, it will pass away. [9]For we know in part and we prophesy in part, [10]but when perfection comes, the imperfect disappears. [11]When I was a child, I talked like a child, I thought like a child, I reasoned like a child. When I became a man, I put childish ways behind me. [12]Now we see but a poor reflection as in a mirror; then we shall see face to face. Now I know in part; then I shall know fully, even as I am fully known.

[13]And now these three remain: faith, hope and love. But the greatest of these is love (1 Cor. 12:31–13:13).

# I

# The Most Excellent Way

'But eagerly desire the greater gifts. And now
I will show you the most excellent way'
1 Corinthians 12:31

1 Corinthians 13 is possibly the most famous chapter of the Bible. It stands alongside the great chapters like Romans 8, John 14 and Hebrews 11. For sheer poetic, or rhetorical, eloquence and in theological content it could be said to parallel the Sermon on the Mount. Perhaps you haven't seen 1 Corinthians 13 as a theological treatise – but it is. Perhaps you haven't seen the Sermon on the Mount as theological – but it is. The Sermon on the Mount is a spiritual exposition of the law of Moses, the ten commandments, and their application. 1 Corinthians 13 is a description of that law fulfilled. Romans 13:8 says:

> Let no debt remain outstanding, except the continuing debt to love one another, for he who loves his fellowman has fulfilled the law. The commandments, 'Do not commit adultery,' 'Do not murder,' 'Do not steal,' 'Do not covet,' and whatever other commandment there may be, are summed up in this one rule: 'Love your neighbour as yourself.' Love does no harm to its neighbour. Therefore love is the fulfilment of the law.

1 Corinthians 13 shows exactly that: how the law is fulfilled.

The apostle Paul titles this chapter 'The Most Excellent Way'. The King James Version says: 'I show unto you a *more* excellent way'; the New English Bible translates it: 'The best way of all'. The Greek may be translated: 'a supremely excellent way'. In other words, it is the best way to live; the best way that can be imagined.

There is a scholarly debate as to whether or not Paul is using somebody else's material here. There are those who believe that this chapter was a hymn of the early church used from community to community. A similar suggestion is made regarding Philippians 2:5-11.[1] However, I take the view that in both instances Paul is the author.

Paul's purpose in writing 1 Corinthians 13 is to show us the way we should live. I only wish that I had heard my pastor preach on this when I was a teenager. I think it would have made a difference in my own life to have been gripped by love, a long time ago. A lot of us are biased against love because of theological liberals who emphasize social concern; they have taken the word, love, and stolen it. However, 1 Corinthians 13 has only minimal relevance to what liberals refer to as love. 1 Corinthians 13 is talking about the way we should live.

## Paul's immediate purpose

Paul's immediate purpose was to show what true spirituality is. In Corinth there were many super-spiritual Christians, who fancied themselves more spiritual than others because they had certain gifts of the Spirit. In particular, they regarded the gift of tongues as a sign that they were more spiritual than other Christians. Paul shows that there is a better way of judging what true spirituality is: 'the most excellent way'.

---

1. See my book *Meekness and Majesty*, an exposition of Philippians 2:5-11, published by Christian Focus.

It is a missing note at the present time, even with all of the widespread interest in the gifts of the Spirit.

Over twenty years ago, my family and I were having a holiday in Holland, and we went to Corrie ten Boom's place in Haarlem, over a jewellery store where the 'hiding place' that was used to protect Jews in the Second World War is. It worked out that we got to meet Corrie in her home. It was an hour that I will never forget. During our conversation I took the liberty of asking her, 'Is it true that you are a great believer in the gifts of the Spirit?' She said, 'Yes. 1 Corinthians 12 and 1 Corinthians 14, but don't forget 1 Corinthians 13.' Those were her very words. My fear is that we have forgotten it at the present time. Whatever our interest in seeing a restoration of some of these gifts, we must not forget 1 Corinthians 13. Love is the most excellent way.

People have always had their own views as to what true spirituality is. Some think that true spirituality is having an old-fashioned appearance. I come from Kentucky where women were regarded as being more spiritual if they looked like they had just fallen off a covered wagon! There are those who think it a sign of godliness to wear their hair up in a bun. But no matter how old-fashioned or conventional a person's appearance is, they may still be carnal and not have any spirituality at all. Others think that spirituality is measured by how much time one spends in prayer. When I was at Trevecca Nazarene College in Nashville, Tennessee, there was a lady there who wanted to pray all the time, especially when there was work to do! When we had to do the washing up, she would feel led to pray. It was just a convenient thing for her. Others think spirituality is what one sacrifices for the Lord. But none of these are necessarily the true mark of spirituality.

**Paul's ultimate purpose**

Paul's ultimate purpose was to show exactly what the New Testament means by love. It is what Jesus meant by love:

> A new command I give you: Love one another. As I have loved you, so you must love one another (John 13:34).

It is what the beloved apostle, John, meant by love:

> God is love. Whoever lives in love lives in God, and God in him. Love is made complete among us so that we will have confidence on the day of judgment, because in this world we are like him. There is no fear in love. But perfect love drives out fear, because fear has to do with punishment. The man who fears is not made perfect in love (1 John 4:16-18).

And it is what James means by 'works' and 'wisdom':

> Suppose a brother or sister is without clothes and daily food. If one of you says to him, 'Go, I wish you well; keep warm and well fed,' but does nothing about his physical needs, what good is it? (James 2:15-16).

> For where you have envy and selfish ambition, there you find disorder and every evil practice. But the wisdom that comes from heaven is first of all pure; then peace-loving, considerate, submissive, full of mercy and good fruit, impartial and sincere (James 3:16-17).

Paul's ultimate purpose is to show if we are like Jesus.
What is this most excellent way?

**A demonstration**

Love is first to be seen as a *demonstration*. Paul says, 'I will *show* you the most excellent way.'

It is a *demonstration in words*: Paul promises to demonstrate the most excellent way by language. By any account it is one of the most sublime pieces of writing on record; even many non-Christians stand in awe of it. What I want to stress, however, is that these are inspired words, these are Holy Spirit words. Isn't it amazing how some can read 1 Corinthians 13 and never see beyond its eloquence? Just as people can sit through a service where God was present in power, and say, 'I love the organ!', there are those who can read 1 Corinthians 13, and marvel only at the linguistic approach of the apostle Paul. But to do that is to miss the point. These words are the Word of God and they should convict us. I know of a man who read 1 Corinthians 13 every day for a year on his knees. He was never the same again!

It is also a *demonstration of works*. We are not saved by works; we are not saved by love; we are saved by faith. Paul is writing to those who are saved. If they will live this way, they will dazzle the world. Jesus said: 'Let your light shine before men, that they may see your good deeds and praise your Father in heaven' (Matt. 5:16).

But it is also a *demonstration of wisdom*. What Paul calls love, James calls wisdom. Why? Possibly because James, a Hebrew, grew up in the wisdom tradition of Proverbs and Ecclesiastes. We read the book of Proverbs and wonder, 'Oh, if only I could have wisdom like that!' Live by 1 Corinthians 13 and you will have wisdom like that. All of the wisdom in the book of Proverbs can be demonstrated living by love.

It is a *demonstration of the will*. When I call love a demonstration of the will, I mean it is a choice. Every single one of us can live this way. It doesn't matter what our IQ is, or our age, or our maturity. The Christians at Corinth had been saved for four years, and Paul calls them 'childish'. But this is a choice. We must never wait ...whelm us. That may never come. ...the will – what we deliberately and consciously choose to do.

## A description

A fresh definition of love can be quite difficult to come by. A two-word definition is *selfless concern*, and if I had to put it into one word, it would be *unselfishness* or *brokenness*. That is what Paul meant by 'the most excellent way'.

First, Paul describes love as *grace renewed*. In 2 Corinthians 3:18 he says, 'And we ... are being transformed into his likeness with ever-increasing glory, which comes from the Lord, who is the Spirit.' This 'ever-increasing glory' is described by John as 'grace upon grace'. Believers often experience this in church or in their quiet time, for example, when they find themselves going from glory to glory. Often the transition is accompanied by suffering, but all experience of being changed carries with it a fresh baptism of love, of unselfishness. It is like the calm after the storm. It is this calm that is described in 1 Corinthians 13:4-5. Look at what it says: 'Love is patient, love is kind. It does not envy, it does not boast, it is not proud. It is not rude, it is not self-seeking, it is not easily angered, it keeps no record of wrongs.' This is a description of grace renewed. It is not only a renewal of faith and trust, but it is a peace that is devoid of bitterness.

Second, Paul describes love as *guilt removed*, and that in two ways: first, we don't feel guilty, and second, we don't make others feel guilty. When Paul wrote 1 Corinthians 13, he was not feeling guilty. When grace is renewed, and we are changed from glory to glory, the guilt is removed and we feel so good. Guilt is the most crippling thing in the world. It is awful to feel guilty. It is what drives people to psychiatrists; it raises their blood-pressure; it makes them irritable; and it is what makes them point the finger. But when the guilty feeling is gone, the need to make others feel guilty is not there. It is when we feel totally forgiven, totally absolved, that we will find it easy to forgive others.

Third, it is also a description of *the Golden Rule*: 'In everything, do to others what you would have them do to you, for this sums up the Law and the Prophets' (Matt. 7:12). That verse is the most practical and elementary teaching one can imagine: treat people the way you would like them to treat you. How do you feel when people make you feel guilty? How do you feel when people blame you? It makes you feel like dirt, you feel awful. Do you know, God is the world's only perfect forgetter. God keeps no record of wrongs.

Perhaps your marriage is in trouble. There are people whose faces reveal the hidden nightmare of their home life. If that is the case, start living like this. Don't wait for your wife or husband to do it – you do it. It will heal your marriage. There are others who are crippled by hate and bitterness. If they would live this way, they too would be set free. 'Do to others what you would have them do to you.'

## A direction
Finally, 'the most excellent way' is a direction as to *the way to live*. Jesus called it life 'to the full' (John 10:10). Paul said, 'I can do everything through him [Christ] who gives me strength' (Phil. 4:13). In describing love as the way to live, I do not mean that we should 'give it a go' to see if it works. If we expect to be driving a Rolls-Royce within twenty-four hours of 'giving it a go', we have not understood what Jesus meant by life to the full. The way to live is to let them hit

you on the cheek seventy times seven. It might not seem so, but it is the most excellent way.

Not only is love the way to live, it is *the way to lead* for those in leadership. Love is *the way to learn*; it guarantees that we will not be barren or unfruitful in the knowledge of the Lord Jesus Christ (2 Pet. 1:8). Love is *the way to laugh.* Love will help us not to take things so seriously.

Love is *the* way to *let things be.* Paul was content whether he was abased or abounding; he could do all things through Christ. There is nothing manipulative about love; it is absolutely emancipating. We        ree; we set others free. What a way to live! Are we a            Are we afraid we will lose control if we set s

Love is the most excellent w

# 2

# The Language of Love

'If I speak in the tongues of men and of angels, but have not
love, I am only a resounding gong or a clanging cymbal'
I Corinthians 13:1

Throughout 1 Corinthians 13 the King James Version refers
to 'charity' rather than 'love'. This is a rather unfortunate
term for twentieth-century readers, but even in the sixteenth
and seventeenth centuries, the word 'charity' did not mean
merely 'love'. So how did the word 'charity' get into the King
James Version? When Wycliffe translated from the Latin
Vulgate into English, he noticed that the Latin word *caritas*,
was used to translate the Greek word *agape*. So he just made
it 'charity' in English. Then when William Tyndale translated
the Greek into English, he just kept the word 'charity'.

The Greek word *agape* was not largely used in ancient
Hellenistic literature. It was the Christian faith that brought it
in and made it well-known. It is a word that is distinguished
from the other Greek words for love: *eros,* meaning physical love, and *philia,* meaning family love. *Agape* was used
to describe God's love in giving his one and only Son. It is
self-giving love. It is unselfishness.

Martin Luther said that God uses sex (*eros*, love) to drive
a man to marriage, ambition to drive a man to service, fear
to drive a man to faith. The irony is, the kind of love that
motivates one to get married is not the kind of love that will
sustain that marriage. *Agape* love must soon come along-

side *eros* love or the marriage will soon be on the rocks! 1 Corinthians 13 is the love that will heal and sustain every marriage.

We saw in the previous chapter that one purpose of 1 Corinthians 13 is to show what true spirituality is. Now what does the word 'spirituality' mean? We use it to describe a person's relationship with the Lord; how well he knows the Lord. In other words, the more spiritual we are, the better we know the Lord.

Take a world figure, such as a President or Prime Minister, that people recognize or perhaps have met. If a person says, 'I know him!', you will probably reply, 'Do you really? How did you meet him?' Then you discover that the claim to know the famous person is misleading. I can say that I know Billy Graham. But do I really know him? There are those who really do know the President or the Prime Minister or Her Majesty the Queen, but they are rare. The more truly spiritual we become the more we know the Lord, the less likely we are to name-drop and say, 'Well, I know the Lord! He told me this today...', and so give the impression of spirituality.

In 1 Corinthians 13:1-3 Paul describes the various ways that people boast of their false validity:

> If I speak in the tongues of men and of angels, but have not love, I am only a resounding gong or a clanging cymbal. If I have the gift of prophecy and can fathom all mysteries and all knowledge, and if I have a faith that can move mountains, but have not love, I am nothing. If I give all I possess to the poor and surrender my body to the flames, but have not love, I gain nothing.

These verses describe people who show attainments that we ma~~y~~ ~~be tempted to interpret as meaning~~ that they really know the

Lord. But Paul says we can speak with tongues of men and of angels, can surrender our bodies to the flames, can give everything to the poor, have the gift of prophecy and understand theology, and yet not know the Lord all that well.

Why does Paul start this section by referring to 'tongues'? In all likelihood he begins with this subject because there was a problem in Corinth with this at the time. There were those who spoke in tongues and said, 'This proves how well I know the Lord. This proves I am spiritual.' So that is the reason why it is Paul's first example.

Four kinds of language are described in verse 1.

### Earthly language

Why speak of the 'tongues of men'? I can think of two reasons.

First, because it refers to natural language, one's native language. It is when one speaks naturally, and that includes everybody. One may say, 'I don't speak in tongues, I don't have that kind of faith.' Do you speak English? It is a tongue of men. The question is not 'Do you speak with tongues?', but 'What lies behind the tongue you have?' The 'tongues of men' can refer to an earthly language.

It also refers to a new language, because in Mark 16:17 Jesus said, 'they will speak in *new* tongues'. What did he mean by that? Some suggest he is referring to a new vocabulary, the language of Sion. Others limit it to the fact that when we become Christians our language changes and we don't swear, or use profanity, or vulgarities.

Mark 16:17, however, probably refers to something supernatural. It is what happened on the day of Pentecost, when the apostles spoke in other known languages, recognizable to the hearers. So it could be both a supernatural and a natural language, in the sense that it was a knowable, identifiable language.

## Extra-terrestrial language

It is likely that there were those in Corinth who boasted that they spoke in an angelic language. Some scholars are of the opinion that there were women in the church who thought they were as spiritual as the angels of heaven who neither marry nor give in marriage, and therefore were too spiritual to have sex with their husbands. Some think that Paul is using the word in a double sense: affirming that it is an unusual language, but reminding us that there were those who talked in tongues of angels because they were already in heaven.

There are three things about this extra-terrestrial language. First, it refers to a *remarkable* language. Paul means literally an angelic language which occurs when a person is carried beyond this realm, and begins to speak in a different language. When that happens, the speaker has no idea what he or she is saying. It is conversing the way an angel speaks. After all, there is a language spoken in heaven. Whether or not it is Hebrew, I cannot say.

Anyway, Paul hints that some speak in this heavenly language, but says, surprisingly, that we can do even that, and not have love. But surely if we were to speak like that we must be spiritual? Wrong, and here is the reason why: 'God's gifts and his call are irrevocable' (Rom. 11:29). That means that God gives gifts permanently. Why can an immoral minister keep on preaching? Because he has got a gift for preaching. King Saul, after God gave the kingdom to David, continued to prophesy, because he had a gift; he didn't lose it (1 Sam. 19:23f.). It may be that God might give to some a gift of speaking in an angelic tongue, but it is no guarantee of spirituality.

'Tongues of angels' could refer to *preaching,* for often that comes from beyond this world. It can be incredibly powerful and persuasive, and the only explanation is that it is from another world. Our gospel was born at the throne of grace, and the content of preaching has no earthly explanation if it is true preaching. It is a message that comes from beyond and defies natural explanation. But it is possible for such preaching to be done without love.

This extra-terrestrial language may refer to a *prayer* language. There have been times when I wanted this so much I was in agony. I would read Romans 8:26, 'the Spirit groans', and think, 'Oh, if I could just say what I mean, even if I don't understand, I would be getting through.' There are times when Satan is attacking me, and I just stand there feeling helpless, only able to utter a few syllables.

Watch out, because you will be tempted, like those in Corinth, to think, 'Because I do it, I am more spiritual than others. I know the Lord better.'

## Eclipsed language

An eclipse of the sun is when the moon passes between the sun and the earth and we cannot see the sun. What is there to be seen, cannot be seen: it is blocked. This helps us to understand what Paul means by, 'Though I speak in the tongues of men and of angels, but have not love, I am only a resounding gong or a clanging cymbal.' Although one can speak with tongues of men, if it is blocked, the person is unable to communicate what needs to be communicated.

Why is it blocked? Because there was no love. It is only noise. Notice how Paul uses the word 'only' here. He says, 'If I ... have not love, I am *only* a resounding gong or a clanging cymbal.' What an awful sound this conjures up – a

clanging symbol or resounding gong, or, as the King James
Version puts it, as 'sounding brass'. It is a reference to the
percussion in an orchestra. Some think that Paul was making
an explicit reference to pagan festivals in Corinth. Perhaps
he was, but, in any case, it is a reference to the percussion
section, without the rest of the orchestra.

Percussion can be lovely when it is part of the whole. But
if somebody just hits brass all the time, it is not meaningful.
And that is what Paul is saying: 'Though you speak with your
angelic language, you are not communicating. Nobody can
hear what you are saying. What they hear and see is something
that is not very nice. It is counterproductive.' We can speak
in our native language, in a new language, in a phenomenal
language, in a preaching language, in a prayer language, but
if there is no love, it is all noise. It is an eclipsed language; it
communicates nothing, only the sound of noise.

## Effectual language
When there *is* love, it communicates. People can feel when
there is love being shown to them. We don't have to announce
that what we are about to say is love. I always hold my breath
when someone says, 'R.T., Could I have a word with you?
Now, I say this in love...'.

We noted in Chapter 1 that love is similar to heavenly
wisdom – pure, peace-loving, considerate, submissive, full
of mercy and good fruit, impartial and sincere. When that
type of love is shown by us, the love of Jesus gets through
to the other person, and that person is amazed. They sense
the love of Jesus because we did not block what God wanted
to do to that person.

As a preacher, I have the responsibility of knowing that
God wants to communicate to my hearers through me. I can

either eclipse what he wants said, or I can be like a clear window-pane. When I am really under the anointing of love, they won't see me, instead they will be gripped by the presence of Jesus getting through to them.

Prayer-language is effectual when we are talking to God, not when we are praying in a manner to impress others. We must be sure that our spirits are bathed in love when we talk to God, even if it is an angelic tongue that we are using.

There is no need to talk about that when it is real. People never need to call attention to the authentic. There is no sign in the state of Arizona that says 'This is the Grand Canyon', it is apparent to all. When we know the Lord we don't need to tell people we know him. When we speak in love, we don't have to precede it by: 'I am saying this in love.' When it is love, others know it.

> 'Twas not the truth you taught
> To you, so clear; to me, so dim.
> But when you came to me
> You brought a sense of him.
> Yes, from your eyes, he beckoned me;
> From your heart, his love was shed;
> And I lost sight of you
> And saw the Christ instead.

# 3

# So Near And Yet So Far

'If I have the gift of prophecy and can fathom all mysteries and all knowledge, and if I have a faith that can move mountains, but have not love, I am nothing'
I Corinthians 13:2

Paul is continuing to show that 'the most excellent way' is better than the anointings, or gifts of the Spirit, that are described in chapter 12. Many of us, myself included, would be more interested in the gifts like wisdom, knowledge, faith, healing, miraculous powers and prophecy, than the fruit of the Spirit, which is love, joy, peace, patience, kindness, goodness, faithfulness, gentleness and self-control. That seems to be the way it was in Corinth, too. Paul is not putting down these gifts of the Spirit, after all, he himself said that they are the work of the Spirit, and God gives them to each one just as he determines. In 1 Corinthians 12:18 he describes how 'God has arranged the parts of the body, every one of them just as he wanted them to be.' And Paul encourages us to seek them, saying 'Eagerly desire the greatest gifts' (1 Cor.12:31). There is nothing wrong with wanting them, and yet there is something better. Let me give you three illustrations.

I once read about a person in New York who kidnapped a little girl, and kept her hidden under his house in a soundproof area where her screams could not be heard. The police investigation led to this particular house, but when they searched it they found nothing. Later they did find the girl, alive. She described how she had been able to hear the police just above her and knew they were there – so near and yet so far.

The first movie I ever saw was *An Affair to Remember*. The hero and heroine met on a cruise and fell in love. To test the depth of their love, they agreed not to see each other for six months. If, after six months, they still felt the same way, they were to go to the top of the Empire State Building on a certain date at a certain time. In a very moving scene, the man waits there on time, but the lady, in her excitement to get there, is hit by a car at the bottom of the building. They found each other later, but, at the time, he doesn't know how close she is – so near and yet so far.

There is an account of a man who travelled from India to Wales to witness the Welsh Revival for himself. He arrived at Southampton and was prepared to set out for Wales by train. Just before, he met up with some Christians that he knew. They said: 'You surely don't want to go and see that Welsh emotionalism.' He went back to India and never saw the revival – so near and yet so far.

And that is how I see these gifts that Paul lists. If we can speak in tongues, and have the gift of prophecy, and understand the mysteries of theology and even have faith and see healings and miracles, but have not love – we are so near and yet so far.

**Why so near?**
First, we must ask, near to what? Well, near to what was new. It is what the writer to the Hebrews described as the 'salvation so great announced by the Lord, confirmed by signs, wonders, various miracles, and gifts of the Holy Spirit distributed according to his will' (Heb. 2:4).

The supernatural itself was not new, but what was new was the demonstration of supernatural gifts in ordinary people. Acts 4:13 refers to this: 'They saw the courage of Peter and

John and realised they were unschooled, ordinary men. They were astonished and took note that these men had been with Jesus.' What was so overpowering was that a man like Peter the fisherman, who had had little education, but had been trained by Jesus, was, on the day of Pentecost, able to speak to thousands with great calmness and authority and power.

In the Old Testament, power like that was rare, but when it was unveiled, it would be seen in somebody like Moses or Samuel. These were not ordinary men, they were rare men. But in the New Testament, we find extraordinary power given to ordinary, unschooled men and women.

We can also say they were near to what had been neglected. I refer now to the genuine gifts. I am not against these gifts, but I am against the counterfeit. There has been so much happening in our generation that purports to be real, but when we get up close we see it is not real, and it puts many of us off. But if we are not careful, we can over-react to what is counterfeit and dismiss the whole thing and miss the genuine.

For example, the true gift of prophesying has been neglected. We are told that not one of Samuel's words fell to the ground; he prophesied with awesome accuracy. Acts 11:27 tells how some prophets came down from Jerusalem to Antioch and one of them, named Agabus, stood up and through the Spirit, predicted that a severe famine would spread over the entire Roman world. This famine happened during the reign of Claudius. So there was the genuine gift.

I long for a restoration of all of the gifts and anointings of the Spirit. I would welcome them any way they would come.

They were also near to what is noble. Paul says in verse 3: 'If I give all I possess to the poor and surrender my body to the flames, but have not love, I gain nothing.' What is more noble than giving all we possess to feed the poor, or dying the death of a martyr? Yet, we can even give everything we have to feed the poor, we can have this supernatural power, but not have love. So near and yet so far.

## Why 'so far'?

They are far from what really is new. Jesus said, 'A *new* command I give you: love one another. As I have loved you, so you must love one another. By this all men will know that you are my disciples, if you love one another' (John 13:34). This is why it is the most excellent way. Remember that the gifts and calling of God are irrevocable. It is possible that a gift of prophecy, or faith, or tongues, or a sacrificial spirit, can be manifest in our lives and yet we can hold a grudge against our brothers and sisters. John 13:34 demands three things.

First, it demands what I call a collective brokenness. Jesus poured water into a basin and washed his disciples' feet, drying them with the towel that was wrapped around him. Washing one another's feet is a sign of lowliness. It isn't clear if this is to be practised.

Once I was pastor of a church in Ohio which believed in practising foot-washing, although they didn't do it very often. There came a time when certain men in the church turned against me, because I was preaching doctrines of grace. Hoping it would result in a breakthrough I brought out a bowl of water and said to those who were against me, 'I want to wash your feet.' The first one said, 'I don't want you to do it because my feet are dirty.' The second one said, 'We only do that on New Year's Eve!' And so it went on. Finally, I got one person to take off his shoe and allow me to wash one of his feet, and then some of the others finally let me. I thought it would bring about a breakthrough, but it didn't! But I was so desperate it seemed worth trying.

I am not suggesting that we all become foot-washers, but we all need a real spirit of brokenness. What Jesus was doing was to bring all of the disciples to a collective brokenness.

But there is a second thing about this love seen in John 13: it is a chosen behaviour. Jesus initiated this washing of feet, and we are told in Philippians 2:5 that 'Your attitude should be the same as that of Christ Jesus'. Although he was God, he humbled himself and became obedient to death – even death on a cross! Tha                        he love described in 1 Corint               y, 'I am praying God will giv                            hoping somebody will lay hands on me and I will be slain in the Spirit.' That will not bring about this love. It is something we *choose* to do: we *choose* to forgive, we *choose* to be lowly, we *choose* to be broken, and we *choose not* to keep a record of wrongs. But we can also *choose* to hold a grudge, to walk on the other side of the street, to avoid that person. It is a *chosen* behaviour; it is not passive. It is not something that just happens to us. It is a choice.

There is a third aspect to this love: it is a concealed brilliance. The most brilliant exhibition of brilliance in the history of the world was Jesus hanging on the cross. But at the time he looked foolish and was the object of ridicule. It was concealed brilliance. We are told in Luke 23:9 that Herod was very anxious to meet Jesus, for he hoped to see a miracle performed by him. Although he asked Jesus many questions, Jesus gave him no answer. We may say, 'That wasn't being very smart! Herod had a lot of authority.' But Jesus gave no answer. Everything Jesus did over the next several hours was sheer brilliance, but nobody thought so then. The truth is, being like Jesus is so brilliant that it is awesome, although people may not think so at the time. This is what Paul is after, this brokenness, this chosen behaviour, this concealed brilliance.

Spiritual gifts may be manifest in our lives, but we can still be far from love. If we speak in tongues but don't have love, we are a resounding gong or a banging, crashing cymbal. In other words, it is counter-productive. Why so far? Because of what it reveals about us. If we do not have love, we *are* nothing. No matter how dazzling our gifts, without love we are nothing. So near and yet so far.

Many times we think God only wants us if we are useful to him, and he is only equipping us so that we can do something for him. We find it hard to imagine that he may just want to do something for us, especially in situations of old age or illness, where we feel we can no longer be used by him. Remember what happened to Elijah in 1 Kings 19: God was not in the wind or in the earthquake or in the fire. But he came in a gentle whisper. Why did God not come like this to Elijah before, when he was preaching, for example? Because this was just for Elijah, as a person. Sometimes on a Monday morning I look at the text on which I preached on the previous day and I think, 'Oh, *that's* what that verse means! Lord, why didn't you give me that earlier, so I could have preached it yesterday?' And the Lord says, 'That's just for you!' This love is not only so that the world can see what the church could be like, but because God wants you to have what love can do for you *as a person*.

Any restoration of the supernatural that isn't accompanied by collective brokenness, is a case of being so near and yet so far.

# 4

# Brokenness

'If I have the gift of prophecy and can fathom all mysteries and all knowledge, and if I have a faith that can move mountains, but have not love, I am nothing. If I give all I possess to the poor and surrender my body to the flames, but have not love, I gain nothing'
1 Corinthians 13:2-3.

Over twenty-three years ago I discovered the writings of the great William Perkins (1558-1602). One of his treatises concerned how far the reprobate can go in showing certain signs of grace, and still not be saved. This was a typical line of William Perkins.

This is the principle that Paul is putting forward in 1 Corinthians 13. He is not speaking of the counterfeit, however, but rather is showing how far a Christian who is saved can go in gifts, in anointings, in having those attractive attributes which dazzle people, and not have love.

In verses 2-3 Paul is showing how it is theoretically possible for a person to be saved and endowed with gifts such as prophecy, knowledge and faith, to live a life of sacrifice, but not have love.

Love is selfless concern, and I am sure that is a valid definition of love. We have already seen that what Paul means in 1 Corinthians 13 is 'unselfishness'. But another valid definition is brokenness; this definition fits the point Paul is making when he shows what is missing when we do not love. In verse 1, he is referring to *speaking*. 'Though I *speak* with the tongues of men and of angels, but have not love, I am only a clanging gong or a resounding cymbal.'

In verse 2, he is referring to *seeing*: 'the gift of prophecy', seeing into people's lives, the ability to 'fathom all mysteries and all knowledge', or to see what God will do, 'have a faith that can move mountains' – we may have all this, but if we 'have not love, [we are] nothing'. Verse 3 refers to *sharing*: 'If I give all I possess to the poor and surrender my body to the flames, but have not love, I gain nothing.'

## Brokenness – the missing piece

Now the question is, what is missing? Why should tongues come across as a resounding gong? Why should the gifts or anointings of the Spirit expose us as fakes? Why should extreme gestures of sacrifice, gain nothing? What is the reason? It is the *absence of brokenness.*

What do we mean by 'brokenness'? It is when our pride has been slain, and our ego put to death. And so what Paul is saying is that these gifts, these anointings, without brokenness, will render our ministry counter-productive. It is when our anointing backfires. We will come back to this later but first, I would like us to look at the relationship between the gifts of the Spirit and the fruit of the Spirit.

## The gifts and the fruit of the Spirit

### *Their similarities*

This passage at the beginning of 1 Corinthians 13 shows the relationship between the gifts and the fruit. There are many similarities and differences. We will look at these in turn. First, they are alike in that both are true anointings of the Spirit. If you have got the gift of prophecy, that is a sovereign anointing; the Spirit gives gifts just as he determines. And yet, if one demonstrates the fruit of the Spirit, that is also a wonderful anointing. This is what Paul wanted for the Galatians: 'My dear children, for whom I am again in the pains of childbirth until Christ is formed in you' (Gal. 4:19). Now, if you had a choice between having the gift of prophecy or to have Christ be formed in you, which would you want? What does it mean to have Christ formed in us? It means that we manifest joy, peace, love, suffering. We may not have the ability to heal people by prayer but we would have love, joy and peace. Which do you want? It is a hard choice to make, but, the point is that they are alike in that both are anointings.

The gifts of the Spirit and the fruits of the Spirit are both auxiliary, that is, they are in *addition* to being saved. For example, when Paul talks about having the faith to move mountains, he is not talking about the faith that justified and made him righteous before God; he is not talking about conversion. No, we are justified by faith, and faith counts for righteousness, that is the way we are converted. But here he is talking about a different kind of faith, something that is auxiliary to conversion. It is what the writer to the Hebrews is describing: 'who through faith conquered kingdoms, administered justice, and gained what was promised; who shut the mouths of lions, quenched the fury of the flames, and escaped the edge of the sword...' (Heb. 11:33-34). Achieving faith is not the same as saving faith. So what I am saying is that both the gifts of the Spirit and the fruit of the Spirit are in addition to being saved. The fruit of the Spirit is not automatic just because we are converted. If that were the case, then we wouldn't need much of the New Testament for there the writers plead with us to walk in the Spirit and not fulfil the lusts of the flesh.

The gifts and the fruit are both authentic. They are absolutely real, absolutely genuine, so when Paul talks about the gift of tongues of men and gift of tongues of angels, he is talking about something that is a *bona fide* gift. The gift of prophecy he is talking about means being able to give a prophetic word and being spot on. But this love he envisages is very real too, very real indeed. It is authentic.

Both the gifts and the fruit are attractive. Who doesn't appreciate the authentic unveiling of Scripture, the ability to teach and preach, and understand mysteries. But who doesn't appreciate this fruit of the Spirit, this love. Both are attractive.

Both are awesome. They dazzle the world. It is an astonishing thing to see such gifts in operation. Think, for example, of the time Peter said to Ananias, 'You have lied to the Holy Spirit' (Acts 5:3), and Ananias was struck dead. Then Peter said to Sapphira, 'Look! The feet of the men who buried your husband are at the door, and they will carry you out also.' And she dies. 'Great fear seized the whole church' and then we are told that right after that, people brought their sick and those tormented out into the streets where Peter would be walking, so that his shadow might fall on them, for they believed that would be sufficient for them to be healed. Awesome. And yet, there is nothing more awesome than brokenness. Think of Stephen before the Council: they said his face was like the face of an angel. And then when they were stoning him, he said, 'I see heaven open and the Son of Man standing at the right hand of God' (Acts 7:56). And later, 'Lord, do not hold this sin against them' (Acts 7:60). Wow! And that's the way Jesus was. Anybody could come to him: sinners, outcasts, the poor – they felt his gentleness and heard him gladly.

*Their differences*
The gifts of the Spirit, the fruit of the Spirit – we have looked
at their similarities, but there are also some differences.
Firstly, whereas the gifts come easily, the fruit of the Spirit
comes with effort. God gives us a gift, and it is ours. But the
fruit of the Spirit is the result of personal discipline. When
we walk in the Spirit, the fruit becomes easy: it is easy to
show gentleness, it is almost natural because it seems right.
But it is the result of weeks, months, perhaps years, of saying, 'No', to temptation, and 'Yes, Lord', when severe trial
comes. Such discipline shapes character, so whereas the gifts
come easily, the fruit of the Spirit comes with effort.

The second difference is that whereas the gifts can inflate
the ego, the fruit of the Spirit effaces the ego. It is interesting
that Paul uses the first person singular in these verses: 'If
*I* speak in the tongues of men and of angels... if *I* have the
gift of prophecy... if *I* have faith that can move mountains...'
and so on. The gifts will inflate the ego very easily, but the
fruit of the Spirit is the crucifixion of the ego, bringing us
to that point where we can say with the apostle Paul, 'I am
crucified with Christ' (Gal. 2:20). I, the ego, slain. And so, we
may stand in awe of these spectacular gifts, but the fruit of
the Spirit is the crucifixion of the ego. The result is that those
around such people are at ease. James writes, 'The wisdom
that comes from heaven is first of all pure; then peace-loving, considerate, submissive, full of mercy and good fruit,
impartial and sincere' (James 3:17).

There is a third difference between the gifts of the Spirit
and the fruit of the Spirit: whereas the gifts can create envy,
the fruit of the Spirit puts people at ease. When a gift is
manifested it can make some feel just a bit jealous. We see
this illustrated in the story of Joseph, who, parading around in

that coat of many colours, says to his brothers 'Listen to this dream I had last night: We were binding sheaves of corn out in the field when suddenly my sheaf rose and stood upright, while your sheaves gathered round mine and bowed down to it' (Gen. 37:6-7). And his brothers said, 'Do you intend to reign over us? Will you actually rule us?' And, the writer tells us they hated him all the more because of his dream. They were jealous of him. Joseph's gift was authentic – there was no question about it. There was nothing wrong with Joseph's gift, but there was a lot wrong with Joseph. He needed to be broken. He had to wait a long, long time, before the prophecy that came through his dream was fulfilled. And it is my guess, that during that time, Joseph had to be broken. And the proof of his brokenness is seen in Genesis 45, when he saw his brothers, twenty-two years later in Egypt, were scared to death of him, he told them not to be distressed for everything that happened was arranged by God. Finally they believed him and they began to weep. They saw the spirit of the man. Now the point is that gifts can create envy, but the fruit of the Spirit puts people at ease.

The fourth difference between the gifts and the fruit is that the gifts have an immediate effect; whereas the fruit of the Spirit has an ultimate effect. The gifts of the Spirit get quick results, but the fruit of the Spirit may take a lot of time. Months after Stephen was stoned to death, Saul of Tarsus began to think about it and he was gripped. Jesus' death seemed to his disciples to be a tragedy, but the eventual result was the means for our salvation. So, a gift may win the battle, but brokenness will win the war.

One last difference between the gifts and the fruit is that whereas gifts call attention to themselves, the fruit show Jesus in the person. We can have the gifts of tongues, prophecy or faith, but they say nothing about who we are as people. Gifts point to performance; the fruit of the Spirit points to what we are as authentic, unpretentious men and women.

### Called to give account – 'I am nothing'

Brokenness refers to the authentic person, rather than to an awesome performance. Why is it that Paul says, 'I *am* nothing'? What does he mean? He is showing what he is as a person. For example, we may think our doctor is wonderful – diagnosing our illness and prescribing the right treatment. But what is that doctor really like, as a person? What is he or she like at home?

What Paul wants in 1 Corinthians 13, is to show what we are as Christians, as people who have been converted; we are going to heaven, and we are going to stand before the judgment seat of Christ, and give an account of the things done in the body. Is God going to ask us to explain how our gift of prophecy functions or whether people thought we were great preachers? No! We will give an account of the things done in the body. So that the gifts, without brokenness, equal zero.

There is a principle at work here: 'God's gifts and his call are irrevocable' (Rom. 11:29, NIV). The word translated 'irrevocable' comes from *metanoia*, which the King James Version translates as 'repentance'. 'The gifts and calling of God are without repentance' (Rom. 11:29, KJV). The word 'repentance' means change of mind. So which of these translations is right? Well, they are both right. No repentance on our part will bring about the gift. God doesn't tell us that if we repent he will give us this gift. No, he just gives it to us. The gifts and calling of God are without repentance. To describe the gifts and calling of God as 'irrevocable', however, is equally true, because no repentance is required to keep these gifts. They are irrevocable. So when God gives a gift, first of all he gives it to us sovereignly, but then he lets us keep it, regardless of what we are as a people. When Joseph was given those prophetic dreams, he wasn't a very nice person at all, yet his gift functioned perfectly. A lot of people forget that the most awesome gift can be on exhibition and have nothing whatever to do with the person's own spirituality.

'If I give all I possess to the poor and surrender my body to the flames, but have not love, I gain nothing.' What gain could Paul be referring to? Spiritual gain; without love there is no intimacy with God. John said that our fellowship is with the Father, but if we don't have love we won't be having fellowship with the Father; there will be no spiritual gain.

He could also be referring to gaining the prize. Paul talks about keeping his body under subjection so that he won't be rejected for the prize. But, if we give all that we possess to the poor and surrender our bodies to the flames, but don't have love, we will want our deeds to be known publicly, so everybody can admire us. Without love there will be no prize, no reward.

And he could be referring to spiritual progress. Without love not one bit of spiritual progress will be made. When we pay our tithes, as long as we make sure people know, we will not grow spiritually. The only time we grow spiritually is when what we do is totally hidden from others and only God knows. Then we get the honour that comes from him only: 'How can you believe if you accept praise from one another, yet make no effort to obtain the praise that comes from the only God?' (John 5:44). Brokenness is when we are content with knowing that he knows. Are you suffering today? God knows. Are you going through a very difficult time? God knows. Sometimes it is right that we share our burdens with somebody; I am not speaking against that. But we need to check our motives: are we doing it in order for people to feel sorry for us or to make them think we are wonderful, or because we genuinely want help or support? God wants to know how much we can take on board that he alone knows about. He wants us to be so glad that he knows, that we wouldn't destroy that relationship by letting anybody else know.

What makes the giving of one's life, of one's possessions, of value; what makes the gifts effective is brokenness, the slain ego.

## What lies behind the slain ego?

Behind the slain ego, firstly, *is the way of the cross*. That is how Jesus did it. It seems that Jesus suffered more in the five days between Palm Sunday and Good Friday than in the rest of his 33 years on earth. His whole life was a life of suffering and self-denial, but what he endured in those five days was the greatest conceivable kind of suffering. He was helpless, nailed to the cross, refusing to defend himself. He was willing to be misunderstood. And on top of that, God hid his face.

Behind the slain ego is *a willingness to be broken*. Salvation works in three stages: mind, heart and will. I am grateful to Dr. Lloyd Jones for this insight. It is the order in which we perceive, get gripped by things and carry them out. It is true with salvation, and it is also true with suffering. For example, the mind perceives it as being the way forward. The heart is gripped by the opportunity, and then with the will we make a deliberate choice. And so, when it comes to brokenness, the mind perceives it as the way forward, then the heart is gripped as we see the opportunity to be more like Jesus.

But there is a third stage: the will. We make a deliberate choice. When the devil comes and hits us hard, and we are sorely tempted – that is when we make a choice for brokenness. Mind, heart, will – it becomes a choice.

Behind the slain ego also lies a *positive response* to what is sometimes called 'external chastening'. Internal chastening is what happens when God speaks to us through a sermon or passage of Scripture. External chastening is when we face difficult situations – when friends desert us or we lose our jobs or fail in an interview or don't get invited to that party. These things can devastate us and sometimes we cry to God, 'Lord, how could you do this to me?' And God says, 'You just blew it!' God would rather have us accept the hurt without complaining, and accept his timing in our lives, and be open to any further word from the Lord.

### What follows the slain ego?

The person whose ego has been slain will first of all be one who refuses to manipulate or control others. We all have a desire to control people and circumstances. If we have the gifts without brokenness, we use them to control others, to have a hold on them. If our ego has been slain we won't want to be manipulative, rather, we will want to set people free.

The person whose ego has been slain will be one who refuses to moralize. If we are truly broken we won't feel the need to teach others a lesson, we will refuse to send others on a guilt trip. We won't judge them, we will set them free.

I will never forget it as long as I live. It was 22nd November, 1987. I came home after a Sunday evening service devastated. I felt I preached poorly. The response was disappointing, so were the crowds. I pleaded with God for an answer. Before I knew it my eyes fell on Luke 6:37ff.: 'Do not judge, and you will not be judged. Do not condemn, and you will not be condemned. Forgive, and you will be forgiven. Give, and it will be given to you. A good measure, pressed down, shaken together and running over, will be poured into your lap. For with the measure you use, it will be measured to you.'

Those words hit me between my eyes. I am a very judgmental person. I do not suffer fools gladly. I knew God was telling me that my critical spirit must stop. I also felt that God was promising me an abundance of anointing (which I have so longed for) were my attitude to change. I began reading that passage literally every day; it is a life sentence. I am not what I want to be, but my life began to change.

The person whose ego has been slain will refuse to mention anything that will make him or herself look good, anything that will bring credit. Brokenness leaves no footprints.

We are all afraid to be broken – I am. I am afraid of what it will cost me. It is scary. I am afraid of how I will appear if I am broken. I am afraid, but I want it. I am too old to live another day without it. May God let it happen to all of us!

# 5

# The Fruit of Brokenness

'Love is patient, love is kind. It does not envy,
it does not boast, it is not proud'
1 Corinthians 13:4

Remember the story of the man who, for one year, read
1 Corinthians 13 every day, on his knees? Perhaps there are
other people, too, who have done this, or who feel inspired
to do so. Simply doing this, however, may not cause us to
live 1 Corinthians 13, but it could lead to the conviction
that goes before the brokenness that is at the root of what
is being described there. 1 Corinthians 13 is surely the way
all of us would like to live. I know that if I did live like that,
I would be a better man, a better pastor, a better husband,
a better father, a better preacher, a better servant of God.
I regret that I wasn't gripped by this while I was a teenager.
To my shame, it wasn't until much later that I was captivated
by this message. I don't know why it didn't happen earlier;
I had a prayer life, I spent thirty minutes a day alone with
God, on my knees. It was a good start in life, but if I had
become gripped by this, I just wonder where I might have
been today, spiritually. There is no advantage in delaying
anything that is right to do.

What we are looking at here in 1 Corinthians 13:4 is the
opposite to the way the devil wants us to live. The devil
wants us to live lives of hate, vengeance, bitterness, fault-
finding, self-pity. Are you feeling sorry for yourself today?

The devil loves it! Are you wallowing in self-pity? The devil says, 'Great!' The way of the flesh is the way of pride and selfishness. There is a better way to live. In Chapter 4 we looked at brokenness, the slain ego.

Isaiah knew what it was to be broken. As a prophet he had been used by God, but, he describes how one day, in the year King Uzziah died, he was given a vision of the heavenly throne and saw the holiness of God. Suddenly he saw his sin for what it was and he felt awful. It was this experience that led him to brokenness, which, in turn, meant he could be used by God (Isa. 6).

Brokenness was also the experience of King David, although, in his case, it came because he got caught in sin. Psalm 51 is the psalm he prayed following his sin with Bathsheba and his attempts to cover it up by killing her husband, Uriah. Nathan the prophet exposed his sin and David was broken. He clung to this: 'A broken heart, a broken and contrite spirit, O God, you will not despise.'

Brokenness through sin was also Jonah's experience. We are told in the book of Jonah how, 'From inside the fish Jonah prayed to the LORD. He said, "In my distress I called to the LORD and he answered me. From the depths of the grave I called for help and you listened to my cry"' (Jonah 2:1-2).

David and Jonah reached brokenness by what I call Plan B, external chastening. Plan A, which was Isaiah's experience, is internal chastening. This is when God just deals with it in our hearts, through the Word, or even through the preaching. Now is the time to listen to him; now is the time for our problems to be solved. If Jonah had listened there wouldn't have been any need for God to have sent the fish to swallow him up. If David had listened it wouldn't have been necessary for Nathan the prophet to challenge him. But sometimes God moves from outside to get our attention. It is far better to let the Word convict us.

The slain ego leads to three things. Firstly, it will lead to a restrained tongue. James put it like this: 'Everyone should be quick to listen, slow to speak and slow to become angry' (James 1:19), because 'The tongue is a fire... it corrupts the whole person, sets the whole course of his life on fire, and is itself set on fire by hell' (James 3:6). A restrained tongue – that is what brokenness will lead to.

Brokenness also will lead to a refined temperament. The fruit of the Spirit is love, joy, peace, patience, kindness, goodness, gentleness, faithfulness and self-control. Brokenness, moreover, will lead us to real tears, tears that just fill up our eyes and then spill over and run down our cheeks. I know we can push the tears theme too far. Augustus Toplady, in his hymn 'Rock of ages, cleft for me', shows the limitations of tears:

> Could my tears forever flow,
> Could my zeal no languor know,
> These for sin could not atone,
> Thou must save, and thou alone.

However, I think that Gypsy Smith got it right. He used to say that there was too much dry-eyed religion. Real tears reach God. We see this in the account of King Hezekiah. Isaiah went to him and said, 'Get ready because you are going to die.' Hezekiah turned his face to the wall and pleaded with God. Isaiah returned to him with these words: 'This is what the LORD, the God of your father David, says: I have heard your prayer and *seen your tears*.... I will deliver you' (Isa. 38:5-6). When God sees our tears he is moved. The apostle Paul could say in Acts 20:19, 'I served the Lord with great humility and with *tears.*' Not many theologians today weep. Not many Christians weep.

## A passive reaction

The root is brokenness, and from that comes the fruit: 'Love is patient, love is kind.' What is the point of being broken? Is brokenness an end in itself? No. The text shows that there is a fruit. Love is *patient*, love is *kind*. The more I looked at the first word the more I was sure I could devote the whole chapter to it, it is so profound. There are two things in these two words. First, there is a passive reaction – patience. Then there is an active response – kindness. Patience is the first-fruit of brokenness. Kindness shows how we *act*. Patience, how we *react*. And so, what we have is not a definition, but two descriptions of love, the fruit of brokenness. A translation of the original would read, literally, love demonstrates patience, love demonstrates kindness. The Greek word for 'patience' is *macrothoumeI* and has a very complex meaning – it is impossible to translate it into one word. 'Patience' is as good as any. There are three particular meanings that I want us to look at here. It means to be slow, to be secretive and to be submissive. Let's look at these three meanings in more depth.

### *Being Slow*

There are five examples of slowness to consider here. The first is *being slow to anger*. Does that make you think of God? F. F. Bruce has commented that the love of 1 Corinthians 13 really is nothing more than God. If we want to know what God is like, this is it. 1 John 4:16 says, 'God is love.' This is the way God *is* described many times in the Bible. These

are just two examples: 'You are a forgiving God, gracious
and compassionate, slow to anger ... abounding in mercy'
(Neh. 9:17); 'The LORD is compassionate and gracious, *slow
to anger*, abounding in love' (Ps. 103:8). This is the way God
is. He is slow to anger. And, when we stop to think about it,
has he not demonstrated that kind of patience with us? The
more we have of God, the less angry we will be. When we
are argumentative and judgmental, it is because we have
forgotten God's patience with us.

The second example of slowness is *being slow to accuse*.
Look at these words from Proverbs 19:11: 'A man's wisdom
gives him patience; it is to his glory to overlook an offence.'
And so the person who demonstrates this *agape* love is slow
to accuse. This is the fruit of brokenness, of being aware of
how much we have been forgiven. Matthew, in the parable
of the unmerciful servant, tells of a person who has been
forgiven, but who then turns round and refuses to forgive
a much lesser offence (Matt. 18:21-35). God doesn't like
that. This is not to say that if we don't forgive we forfeit
our salvation. What it does mean is that when we refuse to
forgive others God is angered and may expose our own sins
and chasten us. But with this *macrothoume*, we are slow to
accuse, because we are so conscious of what God has done
for us, and we thank him that he hasn't exposed our folly.

I am afraid it is true: 'Do not judge or you too will be
judged' (Matt. 7:1). When we accuse, we are mirroring the
devil, because the devil is the accuser. But brokenness will
lead us to feel like Job. In Job 40:4 he says, 'I put my hand
over my mouth.' The book of Job is one long illustration of
how a man was brought to brokenness.

The third meaning is *being slow to assume*. A person
who has not been broken is very quick to assume things and

always assumes the worst, whereas 1 Corinthians 13 says 'Love always protects, always trusts, always hopes, always perseveres.' The broken person is slow to assume anything, because he realizes that he doesn't know all the facts, and in the meantime will give that person the benefit of the doubt. Brokenness prevents us from wanting to jump in with quick answers: it makes us slow to assume.

The fourth meaning is *being slow to advise*. We should be slow to advise for two reasons. Firstly, because we don't have all the facts. A good physician will wait and look at his patient. He will look at her face, at her body posture, at her record, and will ask a lot of questions and weigh up everything, before giving his diagnosis. Similarly, a good judge will listen to both sides of the story before he pronounces a verdict. But the unbroken person is not like this; his attitude is, 'I've got all the answers, I know it all. You can't teach me anything.'

The second reason we should be slow to advise is that people are not always ready for that advice. Through brokenness we will learn when a person is ready for advice or not. Some of us don't want our problems solved, we just want them understood. Instead of advice, we just want to know someone is there for us. And so the person who is broken doesn't jump in with a quick solution but just says, 'I'm there.'

The fifth meaning is *being slow to become anxious*. Love doesn't panic. The King James Version says 'Love suffereth long.' It is the ability to wait. David waited on the Lord. Brokenness lets God determine the time it takes to get the job done. Let God take over, casting all your anxiety upon him, for he cares for you (1 Pet. 5:7). 'My yoke is easy and my burden is light', said Jesus (Matt. 11:30).

That is the first thing about this word that is translated, 'patience': it means being slow.

## Being secretive

It also means being secretive. This word means that which motivates a person so he doesn't tell what he knows. God is like that. We are told that God just separates us from our sins as far as the east is from the west (Ps. 103:12). He doesn't tell what he knows about us, for to tell could be to punish. Some of us are controllers – we like to have certain kinds of information about people because we can hurt or control them. That's blackmail, that's punishing. But God, who knows enough about us to ruin us, doesn't tell. He keeps the secret. One scholar puts it like this, 'Patience of injuries without paying back, the opposite of the eye for an eye and tooth for a tooth.' The mark of love is to refuse to inflict punishment by telling what we know. It is also keeping the secret of the Lord. The positive side to secretiveness is that not only will we not spill the beans on others but also we won't tell those personal, precious things that God has told us; however much they might impress others. Instead we keep it secret, we are patient, and leave it up to God to tell others if he wants them to know of his approval. We don't have to say it.

## Being submissive

Thirdly, *macrothoume*, as well as meaning to be slow, and secretive, also means to be *submissive*. What kind of submission are we talking about? First, that we accept circumstances as being what God has allowed for the time being. And we just submit. We just let things be. Secondly, it is acceptance of the people God has brought into our lives. It could be that we don't like the way God has let people walk all over us. Take Job's friends, for example. The expression springs to mind, 'If that's a friend, who needs an enemy!' Well, so it was with Job's comforters. But God raised them up to break Job. Some may say, 'Well, if I get broken, I want it to be by so-and-so,' like the person who says, 'If I ever get saved, I'm going to get saved by Billy Graham!' But God chooses the unexpected people, possibly even those we think are beneath us. God raised them up to be a blessing to us; they were God's instruments to break us. And so patience is being submissive to the circumstances that God has allowed for the time being, and acceptance of the people God has brought into our lives. Love is patient.

## A positive action

That brings us to the end of this look at the passive side of brokenness. But as we saw earlier in the chapter there is also positive action. Love is kind. Kindness is a positive action. When I think of this word it takes me right back to when I was a boy. I recall how a Roman Catholic evangelistic agency gave three rules on how to win non-Catholics to the faith. Rule 1 was 'Be kind'. Rule 2 was 'Be kind'. Rule 3 was 'Be kind'. Now most of us know what this word means. We certainly know when we are not treated with kindness.

But, how do we show this positive action of kindness? True kindness is the fruit of brokenness. It is more than being nice; we can be manipulative and still be nice. It is more than being courteous; we can be manipulative and courteous because we hope to achieve something. Niceness and courtesy are mere imitations; the fruit without the root. Our word comes from the root which is brokenness. Brokenness – the rootstock of the fruit of the Spirit.

There are three words that demonstrate what Paul means by this word that is translated 'shows kindness'. It first of all means *goodness*. 'For this very reason make every effort to add to your faith, goodness' (2 Pet. 1:5). The KJV calls it, 'virtue'. God is good: we noted that 1 Corinthians 13 mirrors God. 'Taste and see that the LORD is good' (Ps. 34:8). 'The LORD is good to all' (Ps. 145:9). Only one human is described in the Bible as being good – Barnabas. Barnabas was also fearless. He accepted Saul of Tarsus when everyone else was scared of him, but later he differed with Saul over John Mark. So goodness isn't being 'wet', but it is possessing that quality that could be called 'unself-righteous morality'. How many people do you know like that? We know the kind of people, don't we, who are so pious that after ten minutes in their company we want to go out and shoot somebody! Goodness, unself-righteous morality; morality without being judgmental. That is what Paul means by love showing kindness. We can't manipulate that. It flows from within a person who has been broken.

Secondly, this word translated 'shows kindness' also means *graciousness*. This is what Jonah said about God: '... you are a gracious and compassionate God, slow to anger and abounding in love' (Jonah 4:2). We are told that God lets the rain fall on the just and the unjust. He is gracious. Graciousness accepts people just as they are, seeing the rough diamond that others want to dismiss out of hand, noticing the potential in someone that others are blind to. Graciousness puts the intimidated person completely at ease. God is gracious. When we are expecting God to get the whip out because of something we have done, instead we experience God's graciousness. Sometimes we think, 'Oh Lord, I don't deserve to be blessed today,' but he does bless us, he gives us a wonderful day, and we say, 'Oh, Lord, thank you!' He is gracious, he is gracious. He knows all about us, and he loves us just the same – how gracious!

And so, when Paul says 'show kindness' he means goodness, graciousness, and thirdly, *gentleness*. In 1 Thessalonians 2:7, Paul says, 'As apostles of Christ we could have
been a burden to you, but we were gentle among you, like
a mother caring for her little children.' What that means is
*softness*. Proverbs 15:1 says, 'A gentle answer turns away
wrath, but a harsh word stirs up anger.' Gentleness is having
the grace to use our words to diffuse tension as opposed to
saying what is emotive. We are told of Jesus, 'A bruised reed
he will not break, and a smouldering wick he will not snuff
out' (Matt. 12:20). It is sweetness; we read in Proverbs 16:24,
'Pleasant words are a honeycomb, sweet to the soul and healing to the bones.' There is just something about this kind of
person. I am not talking about syrupy, mushy emotionalism,
but just a special quality in the person that makes us want to
be around them. And that was Jesus. People just wanted to
be there. It is the fruit of brokenness.

There is one further description that transcends all the others: the kind person is a peacemaker. 'Blessed are the peace-
makers for they will be called sons of God' (Matt. 5:9). They
are the mediators of the world; they get enemies together;
they don't take sides; they are ruthless in their objectivity, but
sweet in the way they talk to people. We need a friend like
that. Someone who is kind and gentle, but is willing to say
what we need to hear. But a person like that has been broken,
and has come to terms with suffering. There is a kindness
that is manipulative, expecting to get something in return,
but there is a kindness that mirrors Jesus; expecting nothing
but continuing to be good, gracious and gentle.

Many years ago I poured out my heart to Joseph Tson who
came through London when I was undergoing a severe trial
– I hoped he would pat me on the shoulder and condone my

bitterness. Instead he said, 'R.T., you must totally forgive them. Until you totally forgive them you will be in chains. Release them and you will be released.' Nobody had even talked to me like that in my whole life. Faithful are the wounds of a friend. It was the greatest single word I ever heard in a private conversation. His word was sheer kindness.

# 6

# Nothing to Prove

*'Love ... does not envy, it does not boast, it is not proud.
It is not rude, it is not self-seeking, it is not easily angered,
it keeps no record of wrongs'*
1 Corinthians 13:4-5

In the previous chapter we looked at two positive descriptions of love: 'Love is patient, love is kind' (1 Cor. 13:4). Paul, however, moves from those two positive descriptions, to what I can only call seven negative descriptions. By negative I mean that he shows what love is not. Sometimes we can describe what we mean best by stating what it isn't, what we don't mean. And that is what Paul is doing. He says what love isn't and so we can reverse it and assume what it is.

**Having nothing to prove**
Each of these negative descriptions is slightly different, but they do overlap to some extent. In this chapter we will discuss the first six of these descriptions, and go on in the following chapter to consider that sobering phrase: 'It keeps no record of wrongs.' When added up, these descriptions amount to this: 'having nothing to prove'. This will become clearer as we look deeper into Paul's meaning. Imagine a person who, having claimed to be innocent about something, then goes on and on and on in an attempt to prove it. The more he talks the more you feel, 'Ah, there's something fishy here! If you were innocent, you wouldn't need to prove it to me.' The one

who is really innocent, in the words of Shakespeare, doesn't have to 'protest too much'. Don't misunderstand me, I am not saying that a person who is experienced in love is innocent, but what is the case is that when this love is there, innocent or not, we feel no need to state it either way. We are willing to leave it. And so, when added up, and I hope it becomes clearer, we are talking about an internal power that enables us, as it were, simply to keep our mouths shut. No need to prove anything. It is the greatest liberty there is. It is the fruit of internal security. When this love of God is poured into our hearts, it gives us in that moment, an internal security; we no longer feel the need to say anything to make ourselves look better or to prove our point. We are totally at peace with ourselves. Internal security like this doesn't come by external circumstances; it comes from within. Sometimes we need the external circumstances to make us feel better, and that can happen, but that's not what this is. It is the love of God that enables one to experience this internally.

There is, however, what I would call a natural counterfeit to all this. Think of the three rules of the SAS, the Special Air Services: never explain; never complain, never apologise. But these are not rules to live by because sometimes we do need to apologise, and sometimes we do need to give an explanation. Perhaps, however, we should never complain. But living the way of the SAS: never explain, never complain, never apologise, is the result of the stiff-upper lip mentality, if not arrogance, and it can come by the way we are brought up and it can come by training. But what Paul has in mind is different. What he is talking about is what flows easily when the love of God is there. It cannot be achieved by training or by being gentry bred, it is what flows from this most excellent way.

Each of these 'negative' descriptions can be summed
up by a positive statement, by reversing Paul's negative
descriptions. For example, the first statement he makes is:
'Love does not envy.' So we turn this round and say 'Love
is being satisfied.'

## Love is being satisfied

A dictionary definition of envy would be something like 'a
feeling of discontent aroused by someone else's possessions'.
That is what I mean by being unsatisfied. However, love gives
one a feeling of being satisfied. And you see, love does not
envy and the person who is unsatisfied is still looking for his
identity, wanting to know who he is.

Three things can be said about envy. First, it is of the flesh,
it flows from nature. We don't have to go to school to learn
how to be envious, everybody grows up that way.

Envy is also a feeling. The feeling may or may not be
verbalized, but it is there, you feel it. Envy comes from the
Greek word that means 'to boil', that is, with hatred. Often
we won't admit that we feel this way. It flows from our dis-
satisfaction with ourselves and the feeling that other people
are so much better off. Yet when this love comes we just
don't feel that way!

Envy is based on fear. Fear because of what we don't
have, being threatened by what others do have. But envy
is misleading. George Bernard Shaw said, 'There are two
tragedies in life. One is to lose your heart's desire. The other
is to gain it.' Someone else has put it like this: 'If envy were
not so tragic, it would be comical, because it is always based
on a misconception of the other person's position.' So, a
woman might say, 'If only I had her husband, I'd be happy!'
Or someone else might say, 'If only I had his money, what

freedom I would have!', or 'If only I had his gift, then I would be fulfilled!' But love is its own fulfilment; it just doesn't envy. We are satisfied: 'The LORD is my shepherd; I shall lack nothing' (Ps. 23:1). There comes a time when the love of God is poured into our hearts, and we don't feel any envy at all. Ten minutes before, even if we wouldn't admit it, deep down envy was there. But all of a sudden, unexpectedly, the Lord shows up, and we think, 'Oh, wow!' When this love is there it just seems so natural, we don't feel any envy. We become happy with the way God made us, happy with the place God has put us, happy with the way God has led us. That is what *agape* love does for us; it doesn't envy, it is not threatened by another person's position. Whenever we are tempted to envy someone we need to remind ourselves that we don't know the other side. Perhaps if we knew the facts better we would realise there is not so much to be envious of. Envy is always based on a misconception.

**Love is secure**
The second of these descriptions of love is: 'it does not boast'. If we reverse this we arrive at the meaning, *love is secure*. The KJV says, 'love vaunteth not itself' (the word 'vaunt' means to praise). So love doesn't praise itself. Why do we boast? We boast because we are envious and insecure. We know that if we boast we will make the person listening to us just a little bit envious. This behaviour camouflages the envy we are feeling rather than helping us come to terms with it. We want other people to admire us, we are tired of having to admire them.

Five or six years ago I was reading Ecclesiastes in my Bible reading time (I use Robert Murray McCheyne's plan) and a verse that I have often read before struck me with such

force and freshness it was as though I was reading it for the
first time:

I saw that all labour and all achievement spring from man's
envy of his neighbour (Eccles. 4:4).

This verse devastated me, for what it is saying is that envy
is the motivating force behind everything. As I began to
understand this verse I started to search my heart and I was
so embarrassed before the Lord. That feeling still hasn't left
me, five years on, for I began to realize that what I sought
to do, what I sought to achieve, was not totally for the glory
of God, to put it mildly. And I began to think, 'Is there not
a better way to live?'

Dale Carnegie, author of the famous book, *How to Win
Friends and Influence People,* said, 'The two great urges in
the human person are the sex urge and the desire to feel important or to be admired.' The desire to feel important stems
from insecurity, having to prove we are of value in some
way. But Paul says, 'Love does not boast.' It is impossible
to love and to boast at the same time. I am not talking about
the love of St. Valentine's Day; but *agape* love, self-giving
love. It is impossible to show this love and boast at the same
time. Love is secure.

**Love is simplicity**
Thirdly, love 'is not proud'. The King James Version said it
best: 'Love is not puffed up.' That is exactly what the word
means. To put it positively, we could say that *love is simplicity*. It is not arrogant, it is plain and simple. To put it another
way, it is not concerned about its image. We all want to project
a certain image, and are anxious about what image people

have of us. But as long as we are concerned about what they think of us, we are not demonstrating love, because when this love fills our hearts, we just don't care about that. The flesh wants to protect the image others have of us, because of our pride. We want people to think we are a bit different, that we are not ordinary, rather a cut above others, that we are not stupid. Are you proud of your background? Of your job? Of your education, your gift, your talent, your hobby? You want people to know that you are a bit sophisticated? And that you are certainly not simple? But this love means we don't have to prove anything, because this love is not proud. But it is simple. To put it still another way: it takes away the fear of being humiliated, because we are already humbled. Someone put it like this, 'He who subjects himself in love to his neighbour, can never be humiliated.'

The fear of humiliation causes us to be defensive. And it is that defensiveness that will get us into trouble every time. 'Pride goes before destruction; a haughty spirit before a fall' (Prov. 16:18). This is because pride is unteachable. Pride will not admit to being in the wrong. But when the love of God is flowing in our hearts, it is the easiest thing in the world to say, 'I am wrong! I am sorry!' When that love isn't flowing, however, we are defensive. The flesh takes over, and we succumb to pride.

But love is simplicity. Simplicity is so sweet, it has nothing to prove. With simplicity we don't mind being seen as simple or plain, we can admit to not knowing. You can admit to being in the wrong. It is so unpretentious, it is like Jesus. Jesus demonstrated great simplicity in being able to give up everything and become nothing. He had no need to prove who he was.

## Love is seemly

Fourthly, love 'is not rude'. Many contemporary Greek scholars agree that this word used by the NIV, 'rude', is an unfortunate translation, as it encompasses only about 20% of the meaning. Again, it is the KJV that gives the most accurate reading: love 'doth not behave itself unseemly'. To put this in positive terms we could say, *Love is seemly*. To use Leon Morris's words: 'It is in accordance with due form'. That, however, may still need some explanation. When love is working, what is said and done will not raise eyebrows, or seem odd, or be out of place. 1 John 2:10 captures the meaning: 'Whoever loves his brother lives in the light, and there is nothing in him to make him stumble.' 'I put my foot in it again', we say when we have said the wrong thing. The reason we make those stupid comments is because the flesh has got control and the words come out before we know it, and we think, 'Oh! Why did I ever say that!' But when we are governed by love, we just don't make those kind of stupid comments.

To put it another way: love doesn't shock, or love doesn't embarrass. It doesn't do what is regarded as improper. It is interesting to note that this same word is used in 1 Corinthians 7:36: 'If anyone thinks he is acting improperly towards the virgin he is engaged to...'. The NIV's translation 'isn't rude' is true in part, but doesn't capture the whole meaning. Love doesn't behave shamefully or disgracefully, untactfully or embarrassingly. It is seemly. There is an old saying that you can spot a gentleman not by the way he addresses his king, but by the way he addresses his servants. And so, this love when it is in action is at home with anybody anywhere and seeks to put people at ease. This includes how we behave towards the opposite sex. We will not do or say anything that will raise eyebrows, or embarrass. Someone governed by this love, even if he isn't a cultured person, shows culture and dignity.

## Love is selfless

Fifthly, love 'is not self-seeking', or, in the words of the KJV, love 'seeketh not her own'. In other words, *love is selfless*. 'Each of you should look not only to your own interests, but also to the interests of others' (Phil. 2:4). 'In honour prefer one another' (Rom. 12:10). 'Christ pleased not himself' (Rom. 15:3). It is devoid of vain ambition. It means we won't pull strings to get where we want to go. We will let God put us there. Someone summed this up well in the words: 'Love does not merely not seek that which does not belong to it, it is prepared to give up for the sake of others even what it is entitled to.' Paul said:

> Your attitude should be the same as that of Christ Jesus:
>     Who, being in very nature God,
>         did not consider equality with God
>             something to be grasped,
>     but made himself nothing,
>         taking the very nature of a servant,
>         being made in human likeness.
>     And being found in appearance as a man,
>         he humbled himself
>         and became obedient to death –
>             even death on a cross
>                                                    (Phil. 2:5-8).

And so, when it comes to personal interests, we let them go. This message must have hit the Corinthians right between the eyes, for only a few chapters earlier we read that they were taking one another to court to get what was coming to them (1 Cor. 6) and were eating meat that had been sacrificed to idols in front of weaker Christians (1 Cor. 8). It didn't bother them, but was a stumbling block to others. The flesh says, 'I want my rights,' but love gives it all up.

## Love is serene

Sixthly, love 'is not easily angered'. This could be summed up positively as: *love is serene*. J. B. Phillips translates it, 'Love is not touchy.' Some of us keep a finger on the trigger and the least thing brings us to irritability. We are impatient with mediocrity, impatient with disappointment, unable to cope with accusations, and so on. The noun form of this word is used in Acts 15:39 to describe how Barnabas and Paul had such a sharp disagreement that they parted company. We are not sure who was right, but we know both were wrong. The love wasn't there. Love doesn't react that way; there is no need to raise your voices, no need to say anything. One of the most amazing demonstrations of this is when, in the face of all the accusations and taunting our Lord said nothing in return. But instead he prayed, 'Father, forgive them, for they don't know what they are doing' (Luke 23:34).

This is love. It won't do for us to defend ourselves because we haven't lived this way. When we are in the flesh, we want to be defensive and prove how spiritual we are, prove how innocent we are, and prove we are not like other people; we are different. When this love comes alongside, we no longer feel the need to act like this any more. May God grant that we won't justify ourselves but accuse ourselves and pray that he will bring us to live this way day and night.

# 7

# The Art of Forgetting (1)

'Love ... keeps no record of wrongs'
1 Corinthians 13:5

The focus of this chapter is on the seventh negative description of love: 'it keeps no record of wrongs'. This message is particularly relevant to anyone whose marriage is in trouble, or who has got a problem with forgiving an abusive, unjust parent, or whose boss is difficult to work with. Whatever the cause of our resentment this message is for us.

Love keeps no record of wrongs. The KJV translates this: 'Love thinketh no evil', which is not the best translation. The NIV is more correct and helpful here. One question I want to answer is why the NIV and KJV differ so greatly here.

What happened was that Wycliffe, who translated the Bible into English before the KJV was translated, based his translation on the Latin Bible, the Vulgate as it is called because it was made for the common people. The Latin *caritas*, for example, was translated *charity*, and it has stuck over the years. In this phrase from 1 Corinthians 13:5, the Latin is *non cogitat malum*, 'thinks no evil', and therefore it was translated, 'Love thinketh no evil'. But a closer look at the Greek shows two things: first, the word, *logizomai*, is the same word that Paul uses, to show the teaching of what we call 'imputed righteousness' (that is, when we believe on Christ, God imputes – that means 'reckons' or 'puts to our credit' – the very righteousness of Jesus). So when we transfer our trust from our good works to what Jesus did for us on the cross, God transfers to us all that Jesus did for us on the cross, and it is put to our credit. For example, 'Abraham believed God and it was *credited* to him' (Rom. 4:3); 'to the man who does not work but trusts God, who justifies the wicked, his faith is *credited* as righteousness' (Rom. 4:5); or 'Blessed is the man whose sin the Lord will never *count against* him' (Rom. 4:8). This word means, therefore, that love does not impute, it does not charge the person with the wrong that is there. The wrong is there, but we just don't charge the person with it.

The second point about the Greek is that there is a definite article in this verse. In the Greek it is *to kakon*, which means *the* wrong. So, love thinks no evil, and ignores the fact that there was a wrong. Some think that 'love thinks no evil' means that we just don't see any evil, we are blind to it. But that is not the meaning at all. It acknowledges that wrong took place, but erases it before it becomes lodged in the heart. Love just doesn't register the wrong that is done. This way resentment doesn't have a chance to grow. Few people have reached the place where they are able to see the wrong, but don't register it. Most of us see the wrong, and the seed of resentment begins to grow and choke us.

There are three points I want to look at from this verse, the first is the subject of this chapter and the other two are the subject of the next.

### The kernel of love
When Paul writes that love 'keeps no record of wrongs', he is referring to what I can only call *the kernel of love*. It is what is inside the shell. It is the heart. Forgiveness is the heart of

the gospel, isn't it? When God forgives, God forgets. 'We have redemption through his blood, even the forgiveness of sins' (Eph. 1:7); 'As far as the east is from the west, so far are our transgressions removed from us' (Ps. 103:12). It is as though it never happened. The slate is wiped clean. When Jesus died God did not impute trespasses to the world. There was a double transaction. First it was business between the Father and the Son; when Jesus died the blood cried out for satisfaction, and when the veil of the temple was torn into two, that was the first hint that God accepted the sacrifice.

And then there was the transaction between the Father and the world, that the Father did not impute to the world our trespasses, and that is what happened when Jesus died. Only, this is not ours until we believe. But once we believe that all that Jesus did and suffered is put to our credit, our record files are destroyed and are not to be found anywhere.

Satan, however, is the fly in this ointment. He knows that we know. If only when we are forgiven we could forget what we did. But Satan plays into that perfect knowledge that we have of our sins, telling us we can't possibly be Christians. Satan is called 'The Accuser of the Brothers'. He calls attention to the records that God has destroyed. It is the devil who accuses. God doesn't accuse, but if I accuse, I am being like the devil. When God forgives, he forgets. He is the most perfect forgetter that ever was. There will be no shame at the Judgment: 'If we confess our sins, he is faithful and just and will forgive us our sins and purify us from all unrighteousness' (1 John 1:9).

Forgiveness, then, is the heart of the gospel and, according to Paul, it is also the heart of love, the kernel of love. Love 'keeps no record of wrongs'. When we are motivated by love, we do not hold up a file of grievances. How often

we say, 'I'll remember that!' or 'I'll never forgive him for
that!' If we ever say that, we might keep our word, but will
wish we had never said it.

## Love is not blind

We must make a careful distinction, however, for love is not
blind to the hurt. That is why the King James Version's 'Love
thinketh no evil' is wrong. Paul's point is that evil *did* take
place, but love keeps no record of the wrongs. Sometimes
we are so shocked by something that we say, 'I don't believe
he did that!' And before we know it, we are saying, 'I can't
believe I thought they would do that! I don't think they did;
well, maybe they did... No, they didn't do that, in fact the
problem is with me.' And so we blame ourselves for thinking
evil of someone and we repress the knowledge, we push it
down into our subconscious. Denial of this sort can be very
damaging to us and can result in migraine headaches, high
blood pressure, sleeplessness and so on. As long as we deny
the evil, there is no way forward. What we need to do is ac-
knowledge what was done. When Jesus was on the cross, he
didn't deny what was happening. When they were hammering
in the nails, and taunting him, Jesus didn't deny what they
were doing, he just said, 'Father, forgive them.' Instantly,
he forgave them. We may feel unable to do this ourselves,
but it is surprising what we can do. Paul would not dangle
this before our eyes if there were not the possibility of doing
exactly this. And if God will help us to see this, marriages
can be healed overnight.

The kernel of love is to know what has happened, but
to refuse to record it. Why do we keep records? We keep
records to use them, to refer back to them. Why do we keep
records of wrongs? Firstly, to point them out to the person

in the wrong. We say to him: 'I know what you did and what you did was wrong, and it was wicked.' Why do we put it to them? Because we want to make them feel guilty, we want to punish them.

How God hates it when we do that! We are asking God to move to one side, and let us get on with it. We are robbing God of the opportunity of doing what he does best: vindication. God doesn't like it when we are hurt and he wants to clear our names and deal with those who have hurt us. But if he sees us tiptoeing into his territory, he takes it as an insult, for we are saying, in effect, 'Look, God, I think I know what this person needs, and I can upstage you and do it better than you.' God doesn't like that at all! When we keep a record of wrongs because we want to use that knowledge one day to punish someone, we are taking God's privilege away from him.

Secondly, we keep records as a way of protecting ourselves. When we put down another person it is in the hope that we will look a little better. It is a defence-mechanism to ensure our own credibility is not diminished. But we only hurt ourselves. Nine times out of ten the other person sees it straightaway. If only we would leave it up to God. In his own time he could clear our names so brilliantly, we would not believe it. His vindication is beyond the scope of our dreams. But so many of us don't get to see that happen because we roll up our sleeves and we do it ourselves, and in too many cases, the world never sees what it would have been like had God been given the privilege of doing what he does best.

Think of the account of Joseph in Genesis, when he was about to reveal his true identity to the brothers who had been so unkind: Joseph had come to terms with what they had done to him, selling him into slavery. Now he had been exalted and was prime minister of Egypt. The first thing Joseph did, when he was about to make himself known to his brothers, was to send every person out of the room except the eleven brothers. The translator was gone, all the court aides gone, everybody out – why? Because he did not want anybody in Egypt to know what his brothers had done to him. He wanted them to be heroes in Egypt, he wanted to protect his brothers. And that is exactly what God did when he saved us. I am so glad you will never know what he forgave me of. He protects me. The kernel of love: it keeps no record of wrongs.

# 8

# The Art of Forgetting (2)

'Love ... keeps no record of wrongs'
1 Corinthians 13:5

In the previous chapter wc looked at what we called the *kernel of love*, forgiveness. There are two further things to note from this verse in 1 Corinthians 13, '[love] keeps no record of wrongs'. The first is that it is the key to love, and the second that it is the keeping of love.

## The key to love

This verse is the place to begin, in order to actualize 1 Corinthians 13. Once we refuse to keep a record of wrongs, something happens. We will discover how God makes himself real. Sometimes we yearn for an experience with God, to see the fire fall, to have something happen to us. Well, as long as there is bitterness, though we pray all night and all day for a week, and fast, we will not have the experience of God we want. However, the moment we come to terms with our bitterness and tear up the record so that what we know can never be told, we will find that the floodgates of heaven are opened, and there will be peace flowing into our hearts. When that happens we will wonder how we could ever have been so stupid to keep records. And, not only that, we will find out that what we were holding against that person doesn't amount to much, because we will see our own sin in all its ugliness. Once the floodgate of heaven is open and the Spirit flows, all else in 1 Corinthians 13 begins to make sense.

Maybe we feel we don't want to keep a record of wrongs, but we can't help it. The first thing to note here is that love is mostly a choice: we can choose to control the tongue. 'Everyone should be quick to listen, slow to speak, and therefore, slow to become angry' (James 1:19). When we speak, we get all stirred up inside: 'The tongue is a small part of the body but it makes great boasts. Consider what a great forest is set on fire by a small spark' (James 3:5). The tongue is a fire, a world of evil among the parts of the body, it corrupts the whole person, sets the whole course of his life on fire and is itself set on fire by hell. The temptation we feel to speak may be almost overwhelming, but if we will stop it, if we will refuse to speak, and not tell what we know, that is the beginning. God, who knows what we are going through, will say, 'Good! Well done!' and will release the Spirit and give us a taste of peace. But what if people don't see their wicked-ness? That is not our problem. God sees it, and will act: 'Do not take revenge, my friends, but leave room for God's wrath, for it is written: "It is mine to avenge; I will repay"' (Rom. 12:19).

When we choose to tear up the record the immediate result is the flow of peace, and the wrong done to us begins to diminish, and becomes of little consequence. We start to remember how God has been so gracious to us. This is the way marriages are healed. This is the way relationships are restored. This is the way we cope at work, in the dorm, in the hospital, or wherever we are. 'Be kind and compassionate to one another, forgiving each other, just as in Christ God forgives you' (Eph. 4:3).

Love, as we have seen, is mostly a choice, and we begin by choosing to control the tongue. From there we move on to trust, to faith. At the end of this chapter, Paul wrote some very well-known words: 'These three remain, faith, hope, love.' Why do you suppose they are put together like this? If you stop to think about it, love is really just very strong faith. And Paul is talking about how to get to love, and in order to get to love, we don't go straight from A to Z but from A to B, B to C, and we begin by controlling the tongue. We refuse to speak and tell what we know that would hurt. Then we begin to see that we have got to trust God to do what he promises. Trusting in God means leaving things to him, in particular as they relate to vindication. Psalm 103:10 says: 'He does not treat us as our sins deserve or repay us according to our iniquities.' We have got away with a lot. God has not treated us as our iniquities deserve. When we keep a record of wrongs, what we really want is for people to be treated as *their* iniquities deserve, but we don't want to be treated that way ourselves. Is that not what is at stake here?

We have all done things we wish we hadn't done. Are we willing for God to deal with others as he has dealt with us? Or are we willing for God to deal with *us* as we *want* him to deal with *them*? We want *them* to be exposed, so the world can see what they have done. But when we trust God we leave all this to him to deal with. If we have vindication coming, we will get it.

Vindication is when we are proved right, when our names are cleared, when it is known that we got it right and they got it wrong. Are we willing to forfeit vindication? Are we willing to make a deal? If God won't expose us, then we agree that he shouldn't expose whoever has wronged us. Once we understand this, it puts vindication in abeyance, we forget about it, and are quite willing for God to deal with them as he has dealt with us.

A close friend of mine once shared this story with me. A few years ago, he was in a crisis so grave he didn't think he would survive it. One Sunday morning there was a rap on his door, and standing on the step was a man he recognised who had a prophetic gift. 'I had to come and see you this morning.' The man said, 'God has told me to tell you two things: firstly, whatever it is you are in, this too will pass. Secondly, the truth is worse than what they know.' *The truth is worse than what they know.* When we become conscious of all that is knowable, it makes us lower our voices. This is why Jesus said, 'Judge not that you be not judged' (Matt. 7:1). If we don't judge one another, that is, tell what we know, then God won't judge us. If we do judge, however, then God is free to tell what he knows, and expose us.

When we refuse to keep a record of wrongs three things happen: we see God's wisdom in all that happens, we cease to be angry with God, and we don't keep a record of our rights.

Firstly, by loving, by keeping no record of wrongs, we see God's wisdom, how he allows things to happen for our good. Those who hurt us may appear to us as instruments of the devil, but in fact, they are God's instrument to bring us to love and to brokenness.

Secondly, we cease to be angry with God. When we stop to think where our bitterness really ends, if we are honest, our answer is, 'With God'. That's where our anger is. We may take our anger out on somebody, but really we are angry with God for letting this happen. But when we keep no record of wrongs, we see that God did everything for us. So his wisdom is for our own good. 'All things work together for good, to them that love God, to them who are called according to his purpose' (Rom. 8:28, KJV).

Thirdly, when we cease to keep a record of wrongs we also stop keeping a record of our *rights*. Some keep a record of wrongs for security, and others are writing an even longer list, a record of rights, so that we can call attention to ourselves – 'See, I told you I was right, I was right on that too, wasn't I?' and so on and on. It is just as wicked to keep a record of rights as it is to keep a record of wrongs. God hates both equally. Love tears up the list of our rights. As Paul put it in 1 Corinthians 4:5: 'Judge nothing before the appointed time; wait till the Lord comes. He will bring to light what is hidden in darkness and will expose the motives of men's hearts. At that time each will receive his praise from God.'

**The keeping of love**
This is the third section we are looking at concerning the phrase '[love] keeps no record of wrongs'. In the previous chapter we saw how forgiveness is the kernel of love. Then in the first part of this chapter we saw that it is the key to love. But, thirdly, it is also the keeping of love.

Sometimes we are tempted to ask, 'How long have I got to keep this up?' We look at our situation and see that we have done what was asked – we haven't kept a record of wrongs; we have refused to speak; we have referred everything to God; and have agreed we are all sinners. But the good feeling hasn't lasted. We have forgiven those we needed to forgive, whether it be husband, wife, friend, foe, parent, boss – but it didn't change them, they are as stubborn as ever. 'How long have I got to keep this up?' we ask. Ask yourself this: 'How long has God put up with me?' When Peter asked Jesus how many times we have to forgive, Jesus said, seventy times seven (Matt. 18:21). In other words, forgiveness becomes a never-ending lifestyle. Don't say, 'I did it once, I've paid my dues.' Love keeps no record of wrongs ever again. If they keep doing wrong, we keep tearing up the file.

We read in Genesis 45 that Joseph's brothers were overwhelmed when Joseph forgave them. Seventeen years later, however, when Jacob died, the brothers once more became afraid that Joseph would at long last try to get even with them. It is no use saying, 'Well, I paid my dues, I tore up that record file, but they have been worse ever since.' We must follow Joseph's example and keep doing it. We find that seventeen years later, Joseph continued to forgive (Gen. 50).

There are two things to note from this story as it progresses. Firstly, Joseph kept on forgiving his brothers, and secondly, he refused to use his privilege to punish. He doesn't even want God to punish them. When we come to the place where we don't want God to punish our wrongdoers, we are there. Many of us, as directed by Jesus in the Lord's Prayer in his Sermon on the Mount, will pray for our enemies. But do we mean what we say? Do we really want God to bless them? Sometimes we want to pray the prayer but we don't want it answered. But Joseph had come to that place. He didn't want them to be afraid, he wouldn't use his position as prime minister. He said, 'Am I in the place of God?' He wanted to be seen as a loving person, and continued to let them save face by pointing out that God was behind the whole thing. God meant it for good. He was so grateful to God for he realized that if it weren't for what his brothers had done, he wouldn't be prime minister of Egypt.

Do you want to be like Jesus? Do you want to actualize the love of 1 Corinthians 13? Tear up that file of grievances, and impute to them no punishment deserved. *Deliberately ask God not to punish them.* That is what Moses did in Exodus 32; God was very angry with the people of Israel following the incident with the golden calf. He said to Moses, 'Leave me alone so that my anger may burn against them ... Then I will make you into a great nation.' Moses' genius is shown in his reply: He said, 'Why should the Egyptians say "It was with evil intent that he brought them out .... Relent and do not bring disaster on your people."' Moses interceded for them. This is the difference between Moses and most leaders today. Most leaders today are mad if 90% of their followers are not coming up to standard. And if God came to most leaders today and said, 'I am going to do away with all those people that aren't behaving well and I am going to start over with you,' we would just say, 'Thank you, God, get on with it.' But not Moses. He said, 'Oh no, no, forgive them.' Moses interceded and we are told that God relented and did not bring on the people the disaster that he threatened.

This is Jesus. Imagine how Peter felt after he got news that Jesus was raised from the dead; his last memory of Jesus was when he heard the cockerel and he looked at Jesus and saw Jesus looking at him. Peter wept bitterly that he had denied the Lord and he was so ashamed. But every one of the disciples felt that way. We read in Matthew 26 that they all forsook Jesus. And then they got word that Jesus was raised from the dead. Their guilt overwhelmed them: 'I don't know that I want to see him, I feel so awful, I feel so ashamed.' But then, when they were all seated together, Jesus showed up unexpectedly and simply said, 'Peace.' *Peace. It's OK.* And they couldn't believe it. That's Jesus.

Are you keeping a record of someone's wrongs? Do they know it? Set them free; stop using guilt to control them. You are punishing them and you are punishing yourself.

# 9

# Forgiving Ourselves

'It is not rude, it is not self-seeking, it is not
easily angered, it keeps no record of wrongs'
I Corinthians 13:5

The focus of this chapter is once again on the last phrase in
1 Corinthians 13:5: love – *agape* love, unselfishness, brokenness – 'keeps no record of wrongs'.

There are those who say, 'I can forgive others; I can't
forgive myself,' or, as I have heard many times in the ves-
try: 'I know God forgives me, but I can't forgive myself.'
The subject of this chapter is the fear that keeps us tied to
our guilt. We can be so afraid to forgive ourselves, perhaps
because we feel it is not right just to walk away clean and
the consequence often is that we don't know what we would
be like were we to forgive ourselves. And so we cling on to
fear as if it were something of value. This is the experience
of many people.

The previous chapter closed with the incident recorded in
the Gospels of how Jesus came into the upper room after he
was raised from the dead, and faced the eleven guilt-ridden
disciples. Peter, best of all, knew what he had done, having,
just three days before, denied even knowing Jesus and now
this Jesus, not only let them know they were forgiven, but
he wanted them to forgive themselves. Forgiveness isn't
worth all that much, insofar as our feelings go, if it is only
the knowledge that God forgives. When God forgives us, he

also wants us to forgive ourselves. He doesn't like it when we don't. If you are struggling with this, so am I.

Look at what Jesus said to them. 'On the evening of that first day of the week, when the disciples were together, with the doors locked for fear of the Jews, Jesus came and stood among them and said, "Peace be with you!"' (John 20:19). He wanted them to feel good. Peace. He didn't walk in there and say, *Well... um... where were you*? In a way, perhaps, that is what they wanted. Maybe they just felt so awful that it would have made them feel better if he had been angry, but it didn't cross Jesus' mind to treat them that way. He just said, 'Peace.' He never once reminded them of what they had done, and what amazes me even more is that he treats their denial of him as if it had never happened: '... he showed them his hands and side.... Again Jesus said, "Peace be with you! As the Father has sent me, I am sending you." And with that he breathed on them and said, "Receive the Holy Spirit. If you forgive anyone his sins, they are forgiven; if you do not forgive them, they are not forgiven"' (John 20:21-23). He walks in, totally overlooking what they had done, and starts giving them instructions on what they are going to do. Sometimes we can say to ourselves, 'I have done so many stupid things, God can never use me.' Well, what is worse than witnessing Jesus walk on water, raise Lazarus from the dead, miraculously multiply the loaves and the fish and then, at the last moment, to desert him? What could be worse than that? And Jesus walks in there as if he had never been away and says, 'Well, now, here's what's going to happen. My Father's sent me, and I'm sending you.' He takes it for granted that they are forgiven and makes it so easy for them, that they can forgive themselves. He is not blaming them for anything!

How could Peter preach like he did on the day of Pentecost? Someone might look at him and say, 'How dare you stand up in front of all these people?' But Peter was a forgiven man and he had forgiven himself. Had he not forgiven himself he would have hidden away and thought, 'Who am I to talk to all these people?' There was the Sanhedrin, there were the Sadducees, there were the Pharisees, there were the chief priests. But Peter knew no fear that day. He could have talked to that Galilean servant-girl who knew everything, or to the chief priest, with equal authority, because he had forgiven himself. He had come to terms with whom Jesus was, what he did on the cross, why he did it. And Peter had come to terms with himself, and was a very happy man.

This was how Joseph could forgive his brothers and say, 'Don't be angry with yourselves.' He knew they had accepted that he had forgiven them, but he also understood that they were going to have trouble forgiving themselves, and so he urged them not to be angry with themselves. The proof that we haven't forgiven ourselves, is that we still feel guilty, still carry the blame even though we have confessed our sin to God. Hanging on to guilt that God has washed away. Refusing to enjoy what God has freely done.

The person who hasn't forgiven himself is a very unhappy person and, as a result, is likely to be unable to forgive others also. He may say, 'I can forgive others but I can't forgive myself.' But in actual practice, he probably keeps a record of the wrongs of others. The person who is ridden with guilt invariably sends others on a guilt trip. When anybody says something that is designed to make us feel guilty, mark it down, that person has a problem of guilt.

It is almost impossible to say which comes first – forgiving others so that we can forgive ourselves, or forgiving ourselves so that we can forgive others. I want us to look first at the inability to forgive ourselves.

## Why we don't forgive ourselves

### Anger

Joseph said, 'Don't be angry with yourselves' (Gen. 45:5). This is proof that Joseph had really forgiven them, and this is the way God forgives. When God forgives, he not only forgets, but he wants us to believe that the only thing that matters is what he thinks. He forgives us and if he affirms us, he doesn't like it if we don't affirm ourselves. So he wants us to forgive ourselves. Not forgiving ourselves is anger with ourselves. We hate ourselves for what we did.

### Anxiety

The second reason why we may be unable to forgive ourselves is fear. Regret leads to guilt, which leads to fear. Now there are two kinds of guilt: true guilt and false guilt. Psychologists call the latter 'pseudo-guilt'. It is very real, you can feel it, and so in that sense it is true, but there is a difference. True guilt is when we have sinned against God. When Joseph was betrayed, his brothers sinned against God. When Peter denied the Lord, he sinned against God. When we have sinned against God, we ought to feel guilty before him. That is true guilt.

What is false guilt? It may feel very real, but it is false because it is based upon false premises. Firstly, we can experience false guilt in situations where sin isn't involved. We leave the house and forget to turn off the cooker: the roast is burnt or the house catches fire. We lose our keys, and put someone to some trouble to help us get into the house.

Or, more seriously, we are involved in an accident and hurt somebody. Incidents like these happen all the time and make us feel guilty. But we haven't sinned against God, so in that sense, it is not true guilt.

Secondly, and of most relevance here, we experience false guilt when sin *was* committed against God, and God has forgiven it, but we don't really believe it. Why else would we still hold on to that guilt? 1 John 1:9 is a great verse that we sometimes use to present the gospel to non-Christians, but it is really addressed to Christians. It says, 'If we confess our sins, he is faithful and just and will forgive us our sins and purify us from all unrighteousness.' So, when we have been forgiven, and we know that the blood of Jesus Christ washes away all sin, but we still hold on to our guilt, it is because of fear, fear of punishment. 1 John 4:18 says, 'Fear has to do with punishment.'

When we hang on to guilt, even though we have confessed our sin to God, it makes us anxious and fearful, and can even lead to serious neurosis. A psychologist friend of mine said that it is common knowledge that anxiety is the common denominator of all psychopathology. We are still afraid, still afraid that God is going to punish our sin. Still afraid that God is going to deal with us. And so because we are so sure that God is going to punish us, we do it for him – and punish ourselves.

## Arrogance

Why are we unable to forgive ourselves? We have seen how anger and anxiety can prevent us from forgiving ourselves, but there is also a third cause: arrogance. It may be the result of unconscious competition with the blood of Christ. We would never knowingly try to rival what Jesus did for us on the cross, but if we claim the promise of 1 John 1:9: 'If we confess our sins he is faithful and just to forgive us our sins and to cleanse us from all unrighteousness', and we know that God forgives, yet we say, 'I can't forgive myself,' then we are not appreciating the benefit of what Christ did for the Father through the shedding of his blood. The Father had the benefit, so he is not angry with us. But in our arrogance we can consider our sins to be greater or more sinful than anyone else's sin.

We need to realize that God doesn't like it when we compete with the blood of his Son. If God would enable us to get just a little glimpse into the Most Holy Place, and if we could see how much God hates sin, but what the blood of his Son did for him, that his anger, his justice, his wrath, were totally pacified we would understand why he doesn't like it when we don't accept what his Son did. Refusing to believe that God forgives us just like that, leads people to beat themselves black and blue. In some cases, people become more legalistic, trying to give the appearance of holiness and godliness, but they are guilty, angry people. They are always pointing the finger, and can't enjoy knowing that the sin is gone and that they don't have to prove themselves to God. So it can be arrogance.

## Understanding guilt

So, where does the ability to forgive ourselves come from? First, it comes from understanding guilt. Guilt, by definition, is the feeling that one is to blame. When we blame others, we keep a record of their wrongs. When we blame ourselves, we keep a record of our own wrongs. Remember, true guilt is when there was sin. Here is the way God operates. The Holy Spirit shows us our sins. You may not believe this but he will not linger long in doing this; he just wants us to see it, maybe for an hour, maybe for a day. It makes us feel pretty awful. Isaiah said, 'Woe is me! I am undone.' But no sooner had he said this, than God said, 'You're clean, you're clean.' And Isaiah was overjoyed. When there is true guilt God wants us to see it. The Spirit comes by and he shows it to us. This is the reason why 1 John 1:8, which says that 'if we claim to be without sin, we deceive ourselves' follows from verse 7 that talks about walking in the light. As we walk in the light, God shows us things we hadn't seen before, and then, just when we think, 'Oh, this is awful!' God says, 'It's OK, I just wanted you to see that. I forgive it.' Just like that. As 1 John 1:7 concludes, 'the blood of Jesus ... purifies us from all sin.' So it was when Jesus walked into the disciples' presence and said, 'Now here's what you are going to do. My Father sent me and I am sending you.' He acts as if nothing was wrong. They felt it; they knew that they were forgiven.

God doesn't want us to beat ourselves black and blue over what we have done. He knows it. He convicted us. He forgave us, and he doesn't like it when we hang on to it. False guilt, then, hangs on even when there was no real sin in the first place, or when there was sin, which has been confessed to and forgiven by God, but we do not accept it. Understanding the nature of guilt will help us forgive ourselves.

## Understanding grace

Secondly, the ability not to keep a record of our own wrongs comes from understanding grace. That is undeserved favour. The difference between mercy and grace is this: mercy is not getting what we deserve – which is punishment; grace is getting what we don't deserve – which is pardon. So mercy given means we won't be punished. Grace given says we are pardoned. Some people struggle with this and say, 'Oh, I just can't have something *given* to me; I just can't take it freely.' The problem here is pride and arrogance – we just won't let God do something for us. There is that in all of us that wants to pay back the debt because we don't want to owe anybody anything, not even God. Some of us won't let others do favours for us because we don't want to be indebted. I understand that, but don't be that way with God. Could we ever really pay him back? All we can do is say, 'Thank you.'

Grace, then, is accepting what we don't deserve. Think of the parable Jesus told of the prodigal son. It seems so unfair when the prodigal son, who has lived like he has, just turns up and says, 'I'm sorry,' and the father is happy to forgive him. The self-righteous elder brother couldn't take it, but the hero of the story is the prodigal son. We say it is not fair that we should be forgiven; but the big point John wants to make is that *it is fair*. Why? 'He is faithful and just and will forgive us our sins' (1 John 1:9). The blood of Christ did a wonderful job and the Father isn't looking for further satisfaction.

So the ability not to keep a record of our own wrongs comes first from understanding guilt, and second from understanding grace. But there is a third thing: it comes from understanding God.

## Understanding God

When we get to know the God of the Bible we find that he is incredibly gracious. Peter said, 'You trusted the Lord and tasted that he is good' (1 Pet. 2:3). Psalm 136:1 says, 'He is good.' He doesn't want us to feel guilty. He knows the pain of guilt and there is nothing more punishing than guilt. He doesn't want us to be afraid. We have the words, 'Do not fear', 366 times in the Bible, as Joseph Tson says, one for every day of the year and an extra one for leap years. God doesn't want us to be afraid. His love drives away fear, and the closer we get to God, the less we fear; the further we are from God, the more we fear. Why? Because God is love. 'Perfect love drives out fear' (1 John 4:18).

God has his own style; he shows us our sin so that we may confess it, but then he says, 'Get on with it, get on with it.' That's what Peter was able to do, or he couldn't have preached like he did.

Some time ago, just before a Sunday morning service, my wife and I had a severe argument. I left our flat abruptly, slammed the door, went down the lift – and the next thing I remember was sitting in the pulpit bowing my head just before the service was to begin. I don't know what people are thinking when they see me do this, but I knew what I was thinking. I prayed, 'Lord, how can you possibly bless me today? I've blown it big time. I'm so sorry, will you please help me?' There was no way I could reach Louise and say 'I'm sorry.' The doxology began and there I was on my feet leading the worship. What do you think happened that morning? I preached with more power and liberty that day than I'd known in months and months! Why? I think I know. I had cast myself on God's mercy; there was not an ounce of self-righteousness left in me that morning. I think that must have been the way Peter felt on the Day of Pentecost. He knew he was a forgiven man and he forgave himself.

There is one other thing to note here. Once we have claimed the promise of 1 John 1:9, from then on it is the devil who does the accusing, not God. And with those who haven't forgiven themselves, the devil will have a pretty easy job. With those who have forgiven themselves, the devil has a tough job on his hands. All accusations of confessed sin come from the devil.

## What happens when we forgive ourselves?

The result of not keeping a record of our wrongs is this: we let go of the past and its effect on the present, and trust God to 'repay you for the years the locusts have eaten' (Joel 2:25). It is his job to make Romans 8:28 true: 'All things work together for good to those that love God, to them that are called, according to his purpose.'

What is the result of not keeping a record of our own wrongs? We let go of the past and its effect on the present; we accept ourselves as we are, because that is what God does.

But, further, when we no longer keep a record of our own wrongs, we know that God will use us again. Take David, for example, whose sin has to be at the top of the list of wickedness in the Old Testament with his adultery, his murder, his cover-up. The proof that David had forgiven himself, as well as knowing God's forgiveness, is found in Psalm 51:13: 'Then I will teach transgressors your ways, and sinners will turn back to you.' How dare David think that God would ever use him again? David said, God will, I have forgiven myself. It may annoy us that David could forgive himself; wouldn't it be more appropriate for him to feel awful for five or ten years, at least? How dare he just come to God and say, 'I will teach transgressors your ways.' But that's what David said.

And so the result of not keeping a record of our own wrongs is knowing that God will still use us. This really is believing the gospel, that Christ bore our sins, and that God is completely happy with what his Son did. So we forgive ourselves and when we do it, we are then showing the pure love of God and the love of 1 Corinthians 13 begins to be our own experience in ever-increasing measure.

# 10

# No Axe to Grind

'Love does not delight in evil, but rejoices with the truth'
1 Corinthians 13:6

When we understand that love keeps no record of wrongs, we can easily see why the very next thing Paul said is, 'Love does not delight in evil, but rejoices with the truth.'

So far, we have looked at nine descriptions of love, two of them positive and seven negative. In this chapter we will look at another negative description, but one which is followed by a positive description.

Paul was writing on two levels: the first level is that of divine inspiration; his words are the infallible word of God. But the second level is that of his own experience. Nobody could talk the way Paul did unless he had a thorough knowledge of the love of God. This is a man who has experienced what he is talking about. We don't know if he experienced it all the time, but I think he experienced it a lot. Most of us only have flashes of it, a taste, just enough to know what it is – if only it would stay with us! The nearest we can come to any hope of holding on to it is the degree to which we could be given grace all the time, never to keep a record of a wrong. As we have seen, that is the key to love, the heart of love – forgiveness.

What we have in verse 6 is the immediate result of not keeping a record of wrongs. If we could never keep a record of wrongs, then we would know how it is possible to rejoice, not in iniquity, not in evil, but in the truth.

It is interesting to compare the different translations of this verse. The King James Version says 'Love rejoices not in iniquity'; the New English Bible says, 'It does not gloat over men's sins'; the Revised Standard Version says, 'does not rejoice at wrong, but rejoices in the right', which captures the meaning. Remember, 1 Corinthians 13 is a description of the pure love of God, and when we experience it, even if it is only a flash, we have had a taste of the way God is *all the time*. When we lapse back into the flesh and don't feel this love any longer, our immediate reaction is that God is now feeling as we do – bitter, angry, aware of others' wrongs and so on. But God does not change: he stays the same, 'In him is no darkness at all' (1 John 1:5). This is exactly what Jesus is like, which is why he could say, 'Anyone who has seen me has seen the Father' (John 14:9). And so this love, in a word, is Christ's likeness. It is the way Jesus is all the time. Jesus did not rejoice at wrong, but rejoiced at the right. He did not gloat over other people's sins.

What we see in this verse is a further dimension of love. Whoever lives like this is a remarkable person. The more I read this passage, the more convicted I become of my own shortcomings.

## A diagnosis of the human condition

What is a diagnosis? It is a statement of the nature of a disease, of what is wrong. What we have in this verse is the apostle's implicit diagnosis of man: what man is like, naturally; what the flesh is like; what nature is like. In other words, what man is like when left to himself. The diagnosis is, he delights in what is wrong. That is what man is like.

This, really, is the opposite of love. It is hate, and that is how man is naturally. We will never come to love accidentally, but hate we are born with, it just oozes out.

Paul does not say that unregenerate man doesn't rejoice – whoever said that people who hate don't rejoice, whoever said that people who are in the flesh don't rejoice – 'Sweet are the pleasures of sin for a season', as someone said. It is wrong to assume that unsaved people don't enjoy what they do – many do enjoy what they do and they rejoice. But what is it they rejoice in? They rejoice in what is wrong, in what is in their own interest. David said, 'In sin did my mother conceive me' (Ps. 51:5, KJV); 'From birth the wicked ... speak lies' (Ps. 58:3). We don't need training in how to tell a lie. We don't need training in how to love darkness rather than light.

To put this another way, fallen man mirrors the character of the devil. According to Jesus the devil's character can be summed up in two ways: hate and lies. Jesus said, 'You belong to your father, the devil, and you want to carry out your father's desire. He was a murderer from the beginning, not holding to the truth, for there is no truth in him. When he lies, he speaks his native language, for he is a liar and the father of lies' (John 8:44). Masquerading as an angel of light, the devil will slip alongside us and before we know it he will make us feel that hate is truth, that hate is justified, that God feels as we do. We need to be wise to this. Love does not rejoice in evil; the devil does. The devil rejoiced when man fell in the garden of Eden; the devil rejoiced when Cain slew his brother; the devil rejoiced when, in Noah's day, man's heart was evil, continually; the devil rejoiced when David fell; the devil rejoiced when Jesus was crucified. Think of how the father of lies approached Eve in the garden:

He said to the woman, 'Did God really say, "You must not eat from any tree in the garden?"' The woman said to the serpent, 'We may eat fruit from the trees in the garden, but God did say, "You must not eat fruit from the tree that is in the middle of the garden, and you must not touch it, or you will die."' 'You will not surely die,' the serpent said to the woman. 'For God knows that when you eat of it your eyes will be opened, and you will be like God, knowing good and evil' (Gen. 3:1-4).

Eve fell for the devil's lies: 'When the woman saw that the fruit of the tree was good for food and pleasing to the eye, and also desirable for gaining wisdom, she took some and ate it.'

So the devil is controlled by unbelief, and maintains unbelief, and therefore, will do anything he can to cause unbelief in us. Whatever is the opposite of God – that is the devil. God is love – the devil is hate; God is truth – the devil is lies. Therefore, hate, flesh, lies, they all are similar, so that when we rejoice in what is wrong, or gloat when someone is toppled, we are mirroring the very way the devil looks at it. How do we react when we hear of someone being overtaken in a fault? Do we enjoy it and gossip about it? You may protest that you would never rejoice when somebody is overtaken in a fault, but what if it were somebody you don't like? What if it were your enemy? Would it make you feel good, or would it make you feel bad?

I remember talking once with two Presbyterian ministers. I said, 'Did you hear about what happened with so-and-so?' One minister said, 'No, I hadn't heard that – are you sure you're right?' I said, 'Well, I think I am.' 'This is too good to be true,' he said. What happened was that a minister had gone off with his secretary. Rejoicing in the downfall of others – isn't it awful? But are we any different? Hate rejoices when bad things happen to our enemy. Perhaps someone has hurt you unjustly and you want God to deal with them, so he does deal with them. Does it make you happy or sad? You say, 'Well, if God does it, I can't help it, it is wonderful what he did.' A word of caution: life isn't over yet; perhaps God will deal with you next! Hate rejoices when bad things happen to our enemies. Hate rejoices even when it hurts the cause of God and the gospel. Personal vendettas can become more important to us than the honour of the gospel, and we are happier about a brother who has sinned than we are sad that the gospel was hurt. That's the devil at work. When a Christian gloats over another person's troubles, he mirrors fallen nature, not the love of Jesus. So firstly in this verse we have a diagnosis of what man is like. Secondly, we have a description of love.

**A description of love**
When Paul says that love does not delight in evil, but rejoices with the truth, he describes the person who has made the *choice* not to keep a record of wrongs. When we refuse to impute wrong, then the wrong done to that person will not allow us to rejoice. That way we would be detached and then we would grieve. Let me put it to you another way. Do you grieve at the sight of atrocities on the television news? Do you grieve when you hear of a child who has been abused? I think you would say, 'Yes – these things are awful. They make me angry.' Imagine, however, hearing of a disaster where a large number of people were killed, and, numbered among the dead, is someone who has not been very nice to you. Would you be as detached then? Had you imputed no wrong to that person, you would view that person no differently from any other victim; you would grieve for him. When we keep no record of wrongs, it means that the record

is torn up and doesn't exist. We are unable to rejoice when that person is shown to be in the wrong. But if we are rejoicing, it shows that we haven't torn up the record, and were just waiting to say, 'I told you so.'

Love, however, doesn't gloat. Take David, for example. When he heard that King Saul had taken his own life, David grieved and sang a lament: 'O daughters of Israel, weep for Saul who clothed you in scarlet, in finery, who adorned your garments with ornaments of gold' (2 Sam. 1:24). For what God had taught David in those years when he was on the run, was to forgive Saul totally, even though Saul was out to get him. And so totally had David forgiven Saul, that his day of vindication was a day of weeping. This is why vindication is always bittersweet. First, because we will not be able to rejoice totally, and second, because we can never forget that what God did to our enemy, he could easily do to us, for he knows our deeds and they may be equal to anything that our enemy has done. There is no real basis to rejoice when anybody falls, even if God is the one who exposed the fault; that perhaps should worry us more, because we may be next on the list. The first shall be last, the last shall be first. And so, if God is about to expose people, he may choose our enemy first, and then, one day, expose us.

Love doesn't gloat. Remember when Joseph's brothers first came to buy food and he talked to them through an interpreter? The brothers did not realize that Joseph knew their language and so they spoke freely. Reuben said, 'Didn't I tell you not to sin against the boy? You wouldn't listen. Now here we are giving an account for his blood.' Joseph had to slip away and weep. He didn't gloat, he wept.

When I look at the cross, I see somebody getting what I deserve. When I consider the people who are going to go to hell, I am looking at people who are getting what I deserve. And when my enemy falls, I see someone getting what I deserve. So this is the description of the person who has made the choice not to keep a record of wrongs.

This verse, however, is also the description of a person who has risen above himself. By the grace of the Spirit something happened to him and he was given the ability to be objective about himself. He didn't like what he saw and he said, 'Enough is enough.' He is what Jude describes as, 'A brand snatched from the burning, hating the garments spotted by the flesh' (Jude 23). And so a person who has come to see what he is like and how good God has been to him, has entered into a new realm, has risen above personal vendettas. When someone has a personal grievance, he has an axe to grind, no matter who he talks to, whatever he does, his whole demeanour and outlook are coloured by it. We have seen it in parliament, when a former prime minister stands up and everything he says is coloured by personal grievance. But the person who does not rejoice in evil, but rejoices in the truth, has risen above the personal.

Once when I was on holiday in Florida there was a hurricane. The electricity was off and I wasn't able to go fishing, but I did get to know the people we were staying with very well. Once, when we were talking, one of them started to quote somebody. I could tell by the way he said it, that he viewed this person with great approval, that this was a great statement. But as soon as I heard the person's name, I thought, I'm not going to like what they are going to say. When I heard what he said, however, I had to agree it was a good statement! And God dealt with me and I felt so ashamed. How biased I am! If a person that I *approve* of says something, then I know I will like it. But if I don't

approve of him, then I don't want to have anything to do
with his statement. But you know, it is just possible that
somebody you don't particularly like will say something
right. The question is, can we rejoice in that truth, or is it
only when we like the person already that we like what they
say? Love is jealous for the truth, no matter who says it,
whether it comes from Billy Graham, or Mother Theresa,
or your pastor. Love rises above personality and prejudice.
Love rises above what is prurient. This, by the way, applies
just as much to magazine articles or television programmes.
Some things appeal to our basic instincts, the dark side of
our personalities. Some people watch programmes or read
books out of a prurient interest and sometimes they aren't
objective enough to see this. Recently there was an article
in *The Times* about America's sexual habits. I found myself
reading this article and I thought, 'Why am I reading this?
I am enjoying this! This is wrong. I am rejoicing in that which
is wrong.' I began to feel so unclean and dirty. But the person
described in 1 Corinthians 13:6 is one who has risen above
his prejudices and his prurient desires.

This verse, as we have seen, is a diagnosis and a description, but it also shows us our duty.

## A duty to observe

Our duty is not rejoicing in the wrong, but in what is right.
It is not referring to rejoicing in the facts. A lot of people
say, 'Well, the truth is, he got what was coming to him and
I am glad he got it, and that's the truth.' They claim they are
rejoicing in the truth. But, that's not what this verse means.
Would you like it if people rejoiced in what was coming
to you? Would Jesus rejoice if you got what was coming
to you? When Jesus looked down on Jerusalem he made a

prophetic statement about that city: 'Here's what's going to happen to you,' he said. But he didn't rejoice; the Bible tells us Jesus wept.

What is our duty? To rejoice in what is right, that truth wins out. There are three things to remember here. First, Satan doesn't have the victory. Second, we should be motivated by the glory of God. Third, we should rejoice in what God is in. This can get very close to the bone. If you pray for healing but are not healed, will you rejoice? What if you don't get the job you want? What if you don't get the openings that you have been waiting for? What if you don't get the rise in pay? What if you remain single? What if you remain unvindicated? What if people never believe in you? What if God doesn't answer your prayer? It is our duty to rejoice not in wrong, but in what is right, in what God wants or doesn't want.

Do we want brokenness? Do we want to be like Jesus? There is no place for pointing the finger. God could deal with any one of us, and be just. But he has been gracious, that way we can be gracious too.

# 11

# Letting God be God

'Love does not delight in evil, but rejoices with the truth'
1 Corinthians 13:6

In this chapter, I want us to look at the second part of this verse: 'Love ... rejoices with the truth.'

In Chapter 10 we looked at the first section, the negative part, 'Love does not delight in evil.' This is how Jesus is. He gets no pleasure from the misfortunes of others. This is why he healed people; this is why he could not stand it if anyone was hurting. He does not rejoice in anything negative.

Love does, however, rejoice in the truth. What that means is love rejoices in what is right. Perhaps as you read this you are thinking, 'Well, I've been really searched as I have looked at these verses up to now, but this one doesn't hit me because I don't delight in evil. I rejoice with the truth.' Perhaps we boast about our love of the truth, our love of sound theology, and so on, but that isn't the love that Paul is talking about here. Love does rejoice in the truth, I am not questioning that for one second, and in the truth of the gospel, and in sound theology, but, the way the apostle Paul uses the word 'truth' here is the way James uses it in this verse: 'If you harbour bitter envy and selfish ambition in your hearts, do not boast about it or deny the *truth*' (James 3:14), and John in this verse: 'Dear children, let us not love with words or tongue, but with actions and in *truth*' (1 John 3:18). Or as

Paul himself put it in another epistle, written in the face of opposition: 'What does it matter, the important thing is that in every way whether from false motives or *true* Christ is preached. And because of this I rejoice' (Phil. 1:18). The word *true* here has the same meaning as *truth*. And now we are getting close to what Paul means by rejoicing in the truth. He could rejoice in the truth, even when it was preached by someone who was giving Paul problems. Are you able to sit under the preaching of someone you don't particularly like? Could you still love the preaching despite this? This is what Paul means by rejoicing in truth; our personal feelings are put to one side, and whatever God is *in* we want *it* to be magnified. So when Paul talks of rejoicing in the truth, he doesn't merely mean sound theology, neither does he mean the truth which even the devil believes in or rejoices in.

Let me explain. The devil is not an atheist: 'the devils believe also, and tremble' (James 2:19, KJV). So we are not talking about the truth the devil believes in, or the truth that the devil rejoices in. The devil knows truth about us that is damaging. The devil knows the things we have done. He rejoices in those things and uses them to accuse us. This is why the great Puritan William Perkins could say, 'Don't believe the devil, even when he tells the truth.' The devil rejoices in the truth of our past, our failures.

Does that mean that we therefore rejoice in this kind of truth? No, we grieve when we think of anything, no matter how true, that is not honouring to God. So by truth, we are talking about that which is cleansed by the blood of Christ. We rejoice in that which brings honour and glory to God, and that which defeats the devil, turning the negative into positive. There are three things arising from this verse that I want us to look at.

## God's opinion

So, firstly, when Paul says love rejoices not in iniquity, not in evil, but in the truth of what is right, it means we rejoice in God's opinion. Have you ever asked for God's opinion on something? God has an opinion on everything. The one who is motivated by the love of God rejoices in God's opinion. When love is at work, we want God's opinion and we stand back and rejoice in it. That's what this verse means. According to Jonathan Edwards, rejoicing in God's opinion is the ultimate proof of salvation. The one thing that the devil cannot do is to rejoice in God's glory, which really means rejoicing in his opinion. Often we sing the Doxology: 'Praise God from whom all blessings flow.' Doxology comes from the root word *doxa* which means 'opinion'. So, when we rejoice in God's opinion, we can say with Job, 'Though he slay me, yet will I hope in him' (Job 13:15). Or we can be like the three Hebrew children, Shadrach, Meshach and Abednego, who, refusing to bow down to the golden image, could say to the king:

'O Nebuchadnezzar, we do not need to defend ourselves before you in this matter. If we are thrown into the blazing furnace, the God we serve is able to save us from it, and he will rescue us from your hand, O king. But even if he does not, we want you to know, O king, we will not serve your gods or worship the image of gold you have set up' (Dan. 3:16-18).

In other words, they were saying that they believed God is able to deliver them, but if it is his opinion that they should be consumed, that's fine – they will not bow down. Another powerful example of devotion to God's opinion is when God tested Abraham, saying: 'Take your son, your only son Isaac, whom you love, and go to the region of Moriah. Sacrifice him there as a burnt offering on one of the mountains I will tell you about' (Gen. 22:2). They started out but along the way Isaac asked where was the lamb for the burnt offering? I've often wondered how Abraham could look at his son and answer the question. He said, 'God himself will provide the lamb for the burnt offering, my son.' But at that point God's opinion was to take Isaac, and Abraham was carrying it out.

Rejoicing in the truth means accepting whatever God says, through whoever he uses, despite that person's colour or culture, background or accent, education or personality. In fact, God often chooses as sovereign vessels the very ones that get our goat! We may fail to understand how God could use a person like that. He once used a man, we are told, whose clothes were made of camels' hair, belted at the waist, and whose food was locusts and wild honey. John the Baptist appeared odd even then. But love rejoices in the person God uses.

Rejoicing in the truth is setting God free to do what he wants to do, to be himself. Letting God be God, and not even beginning to use his name. A lot of people it seems never understand the third commandment: 'Thou shalt not take the name of the Lord your God in vain.' This commandment does cover swearing, but that's not the meaning. The meaning is that we are never to use the prestige, the weight of God's name and bring it into our situation. Thus, I can never say, God is with me, but he is not with you. That is using his name and I don't have a right to do it. The moment I say that, I have abused his name.

Rejoicing in the truth means not even touching the honour of his name. Letting him be God. Paul said, 'I can rejoice that Christ is preached.' It is one thing to praise the name of

Jesus and worship him when things are going our way. But what if all hell has broken loose and we don't know if we are even going to eat today. Would we then be able to rejoice in the name of Jesus?

What if, after praying for revival, it comes to a church other than our own? What if revival were to come to a church we don't think very highly of – a church that puts little effort into evangelism, where the pastor hasn't even been theologically-minded. What if God decided to bless a church like that? I am reminded of the passage in Matthew 20 about the workers in the vineyard. Those who came in at the last hour received equal payment to those who had toiled all day long. 'How dare he make them equal to us who have borne the burden of the work in the heat of the day?' they grumbled. The employer answers, 'Friend, I am not being unfair to you.... Don't I have the right to do what I want with my own money?' As Paul put it in Romans 9:20-24:

> But who are you, O man, to talk back to God? 'Shall what is formed say to him who formed it, "Why did you make me like this?"' Does not the potter have the right to make out of the same lump of clay some pottery for noble purposes and some for common use? What if God, choosing to show his wrath and make his power known, bore with great patience the objects of his wrath – prepared for destruction? What if he did this to make the riches of his glory known to the objects of his mercy, whom he prepared in advance for glory – even us, whom he also called ...?

God can do that. Love overcomes personal desire, prejudice, wish. Love affirms what God is in.

In the early church, it was not easy for Peter and James to make room for Saul of Tarsus. Reading between the lines it would seem these men found it hard. When a 'Johnny-come-lately', with a mind three times the quality of any of those fishermen, given the sovereign authority to write two-thirds of the New Testament, joined them it wasn't easy for them. In the parable of the prodigal son, the elder brother wasn't happy that the prodigal could be made over like this, and so he became angry and refused to join the festivities. This is the principle: love sets God free to bless the prodigal son and those who come in at the eleventh hour. One day the truth will be obvious. The apostle Paul said, 'Judge nothing before the appointed time; wait till the Lord comes. He will bring to light what is hidden in darkness and will expose the motives of men's hearts. At that time each will receive his praise from God' (1 Cor. 4:5). And love does this now.

## God's objections

There are two sides to rejoicing in the truth; not only do we affirm what God affirms, but also we will object to what he objects to. If God opposes sin, we oppose sin. We affirm his standard, his moral law, and we reject what he regards as unrighteous. That means we will reject what is wrong, and hate anything contrary to the moral law of God, whether it is lying, or murder, or committing adultery, or coveting. Love will not dwell in sin, and love will not make excuses for our temptations.

We can see this principle at work in the early church with regard to where they preached. We are told in Acts 16, that Paul and his companions 'travelled throughout the region of Phrygia and Galatia, having been kept by the Holy Spirit from preaching the word in Asia. When they came to the border of Mysia, they tried to enter Bithynia, but the Spirit of Jesus would not allow them.' They accepted this, because

God objected to it. But some might ask, How God could ever object to the gospel being preached? The reasons are not clear, but God said 'No!' and the disciples obeyed.

So, we affirm what God wants, and object to what he objects to. Jude had an ambition in life: he wanted to write a treatise on salvation. Maybe you have got an ambition in life. When I came from Oxford I hoped to be a theologian of some class, to make my mark, but God dealt with me, because that was not what he was calling me to do. Similarly, Jude tells how he wanted to write a treatise on salvation, but God objected, telling him instead to write a little short letter and urge people earnestly to contend for the faith delivered to the saints, and that was the limit of Jude's profile in the New Testament. And so it is with us – God wants total control.

**God's orders**
This is the third point: love rejoices in God's orders. Think of the incident recorded by John where Jesus tells Peter how he would die. Peter's immediate response was to ask, 'Lord, what about him?' (John 21:21). Peter wanted to compare his own future with that set out for John.

We can be so like this, too. It may seem to us that someone we know has a free ride – a better home and job, more money and friends, and so on. But what really hurts is when another person seems to have the blessing of God on the very things God won't let us do.

Let me illustrate what I mean by this. A minister who is fairly well-known can have a really good thing going on the side, by leading trips to the Holy Land. You can make deals with certain airlines and charge so much per head. I have a friend in America who does just this. From two trips a year to the Holy Land he makes more money than his actual salary is worth. This friend came to me and encouraged me to lead my own group. 'Let me tell you, RT,' he said, 'You could make a killing!'

Well, I got really interested, but God said, 'No!' I watched these others do it and tried to comfort myself by thinking they didn't have God's anointing on them. But many do, and it is real.

Jesus responded to Peter's question by saying: 'If I want him to remain alive until I return, what is that to you? You must follow me.' That is God's order to us too.

It may not seem fair that we have to suffer, and it may not seem right that another person gets healed when we don't. Just let God be God. But the good news is this: 'No temptation has seized you except what is common to man, and God is faithful; he will not let you be tempted beyond what you can bear. But when you are tempted, he will also provide a way out so that you can stand up under it' (1 Cor. 10:13). Happy are they who affirm God's orders, because they love God, who is truth.

# 12

# Coping Under Pressure

'[Love] always protects, always trusts,
always hopes, always perseveres'
I Corinthians 13:7

Why be filled with the love of God? True, it is kind, it is
patient, doesn't envy, doesn't boast, isn't proud, isn't rude,
is not self-seeking, is not easily angered, keeps no record
of wrongs, doesn't delight in evil but rejoices in the truth.
That's all very well, but, the big question is: does it work?
In the time of testing, in the time of trial, does it work? And
the apostle Paul pauses, almost dramatically, to show that
this love of God will not only enable us to be like Jesus, but
also will support us in the time of severest trial. When Paul
says that this love 'always protects, always trusts, always
hopes, always perseveres', it is his way of saying we can
put up with anything if we have this love. I think the best
translation of the verse that I have found, although it is a
paraphrase, is in the New English Bible: 'There is nothing
love cannot face.'

The verse contains four descriptions of love: love trusts,
hopes, protects and perseveres. And these four descriptions
stand alongside four envisaged situations. They are four negative situations that you and I face all the time. Paul shows
how love meets each particular situation. These situations are
listed in ascending order with regard to the amount of pressure that they have on us. So the minimal level, or the minor

pressure, is where a wrong has been done to us. Alongside this Paul says, 'Love always protects.'

Then there is the next level, that of moderate pressure where there is an external want in our lives. Alongside that Paul says love 'always trusts'. Then there is a higher level, that of major pressure, where a worry totally dominates us. Alongside that Paul says love 'always hopes'. But the highest level, that of maximum pressure is spiritual warfare. Addressing this situation Paul says love 'always perseveres'. So, at each level of pressure, we are given descriptions of love, but there is more. We need to see that the grace that equips us for the situation, is that which also enables us to protect, trust, hope, and persevere.

Paul, in this verse, shows what it is like when we have taken on board the key to love which, as we have seen, is keeping no record of wrongs. Then there is no bitterness, and the result will be that there will be no self-pity. He is showing us the benefits that are ours that enable us to cope in the time of pressure. He says, we protect, we trust, we hope, we persevere. He doesn't say we will be shouting 'Glory! Hallelujah!' all the time. He doesn't say, 'Oh, this is wonderful!' Nothing like that. But what he does say is that it works.

Let us look at each of these ascending pressures.

## Dealing with minor pressure

What is needed when we have been wronged? The answer is to show forgiveness. How do we know that? Because Paul says that love 'always protects'.

This word 'protects' means, first of all, that love *covers*. F. F. Bruce wrote: 'Love covers all things unworthy, instead of exposing them or blazing them abroad.' We read in 1 Peter 4:8, 'Above all, love each other deeply because love covers over a multitude of sins', and again in James 5:20, 'Whoever turns a sinner from the error of his ways, will save him from death and cover over a multitude of sins.' So love covers that which is unworthy, instead of exposing it. This is the very opposite of what the Pharisees and the teachers of the law did when they brought to Jesus a woman caught in adultery (John 8). They made her stand before the group and said to Jesus, 'Teacher, this woman was caught in the act of adultery!' Instead of covering the sin, they wanted everybody to see it. They exposed it. This is the behaviour of the self-righteous person, the desire to expose. But love protects. Love doesn't want someone to get caught.

Secondly, the word 'protects' means, love *conceals*. The word is used in the Septuagint, a verse that reads like this: 'The fool will not be able to conceal the matter.' Love, however, hides what is there, conceals what is not very attractive in another. So next time you begin to say, 'Well, let me tell you about so-and-so...', remember you are not being motivated by love, unless you are speaking up on behalf of 'so-and-so' who has been put down.

Thirdly, 'protects' means: love *cushions*. It cushions the blow. Imagine a situation where you have to go to a person regarding something unpleasant. (This is a biblical principle set out in Galatians 6:1: 'Brothers, if someone is caught in a sin, you who are spiritual should restore him gently. But watch yourself, or you also may be tempted.') When we see the person who has given in to that sin, instead of pointing the finger, we approach them in such a way that they know we are aware that it is only by God's grace we ourselves are not in a similar situation. We cushion the blow for them, helping them to save face. This love protects.

And all this is the result of keeping no record of wrongs. When we don't keep a record of wrongs the Spirit is released to be himself, and we find an ability to cope that defies a natural explanation. There is no desire to say 'Gotcha!', no desire to have someone found out, instead the Spirit protects.

If you have been wronged and are feeling under pressure, you may well wonder at my describing this as minimal pressure. You may want to retort, 'You don't know what I am going through. It is pretty hard to take when somebody has wronged you.' The least always seems a lot to have to put up with, but it could be much worse. 'He that is faithful in that which is least is faithful also in much' (Luke 16:10, KJV).

## Dealing with moderate pressure

When we are outwardly in want, what we need is faith or trust. The KJV says, 'believeth all things'. Now, Paul here is not referring to gullibility. Many of us are so gullible we believe anything we hear but that is not what Paul means. He doesn't believe that love is naïve. What he means is that love always believes, no matter what happens. Nothing can shake your faith; you always trust.

We experience want in the following areas: finances, friendships, fellowship with God. And maybe you are wanting in these three areas at the moment. Maybe you are under financial pressure, or are having a struggle with friendships and are lonely, or you feel God is hiding his face and you are unable to enjoy fellowship with God. When we live by faith, but without love, then, in the time of trouble, backsliding is not unlikely. At the end of this chapter we have the words: 'these things remain: faith, hope, love'. Have you ever stopped to wonder why they were put like this; faith, hope and love? They are put this way because they are three progressive stages; it is possible to have faith without hope; it is possible to have faith and hope without love, but if you have love, you will have faith and you will have hope. When we are governed by this love, we will never backslide because we will always believe and trust. I don't understand how or why it happens, but the highest level of faith, which is love, ensures that we will always trust. This is why some of us get discouraged easily; we are not living by love. Some of us panic at the drop of a hat; we are not living by love. Those who are up and down in the Christian walk need to know there is a better way to live. There is something far better than what the world has to offer, something far better than the scintillating things of the flesh or the deceit of esteem and prestige – that is being filled by the pure love of God. For if that love is there, no matter what happens faith will always be there. The New English Bible puts it so well: 'Love can face anything.' Dignifying the trial comes easily, believing the Bible comes easily, and letting God handle things comes easily, when we live by love.

## Dealing with major pressure

What is needed when the temptation is to worry? The answer is fearlessness. Paul says love always hopes, so that when we are filled with this love, we not only have faith or trust, but we also have this next stage: 'Now abide faith and hope...' Someone put it like this: 'When love has no evidence it still does not fear. He who fears is not made perfect in love.' John Wesley, in that quaint way of his, said, 'I'd as leave curse, as to worry.' Now, many of us would be appalled at swearing, but our worry often doesn't seem to appal us at all. But what the apostle Paul is saying is that when a situation is adverse, love does not lose heart. Love enables one to focus upon Jesus, not on the situation. If you are focusing upon the situation, you will feel very bleak and unable to cope. We are all like that at times and have shown that we are not focusing upon the Lord Jesus at the right hand of God. But when we do focus upon him, we get our joy from knowing that at the right hand of God there is calm, there is peace, there is no panic. The situation may look pretty bleak, but when we look at him, we may not fully understand why, but we are able to cope.

I remember talking with a friend of mine who had been interviewed for a job in another country. He resigned from his job here and took that job in the other country, but things developed in such a way that the new job fell through, and he was unable to return to his old job. Things didn't seem to be working out, yet he had only acted as he felt led by God. As we talked he said, 'I have got my heavenly Father.' I never felt such calmness. He said, 'I am unemployed but I have got my heavenly Father.' When love has no evidence it still doesn't fear.

This verse has a further meaning also: F. F. Bruce put it like this: 'Love is always ready to give an offender a second chance.' In fact, we are to forgive him seventy times seven, said Jesus. Why do we not want to give an offender a second chance? It is our fear. You see, love treats others as God treated Jonah. God came to him a second time. Someone put it this way: 'Love puts the most favourable construction on an ambiguous action.' The flesh imagines the worst; love always hopes.

This verse has the future in mind. When we are facing delay to an answered prayer; when we are facing disloyalty; when we are in a disadvantage, love always hopes. When we are being disciplined, and are aware that God is dealing with us; when we are in debt, or facing death, 'hold thou the cross before my closing eyes'. Love always hopes.

## Dealing with maximum pressure

There are some situations where, in addition to being wronged, in addition to being in want, in addition to being worried, the devil himself comes right in and rides on top of it all, intensifying everything a thousand times. This is a spiritual warfare situation. What do we need when we are facing spiritual warfare? The answer is *fortitude*: the KJV puts it: 'Love endures all things', the NIV: '[Love] always perseveres.'

Jesus said, 'Lead us not into temptation, but deliver us from evil', literally 'deliver us from the evil one'. We should never seek temptation or trial, we should pray rather for the opposite. Don't ever go picking a fight with the devil. When some people talk about spiritual warfare, I feel quite disturbed for they refer to it as if it were no more serious than a game of tennis. They say, 'We're going to do some spiritual warfare.' This is dangerous: they will have a problem on their hands. Whenever we pick a fight with the devil, we will have a problem on our hands. Rather, we should pray: 'Lead us not into temptation, but deliver us from the evil one.' Once in a while, however, on top of the fact that you have been wronged, on top of the fact that you are in want, on top of the fact that you are worried, we experience what the apostle Paul in Ephesians 6 calls 'the evil day'. What are we to do in the evil day? Just one thing: stand. That's all. Stand.

The word 'stand' comes up four times in Ephesians 6:10-18: 'Put on the whole armour of God so that you can take your *stand* against the devil's schemes'; 'Therefore put on the whole armour of God so that when the day of evil comes, you may be able to *stand* your ground'; '... after you have done everything, to *stand*'; '*Stand* firm, then.' Why the stress on standing? When the devil comes all that is required is fortitude. All that is required is that we endure. Don't try to walk. Whatever you do, don't try to run. Don't slip and fall. Don't go backwards. Just stand.

When the evil day comes, although we didn't ask for it to come, we endure, we persevere. Love always perseveres. We never know when to expect the evil day, but the person who hasn't dealt with the problem of bitterness, who holds a grudge, or keeps a record of wrongs, will almost certainly collapse when the evil day comes. But the one who lives by love, perseveres.

It is the love that will equip you for that day when the devil comes as a roaring lion, seeking whom he may devour. Are you under pressure right now? How are you coping? If we are not living by love we are in deep trouble. These four negative situations will come to all of us in a matter of time, but what will enable us to cope is living by love. And that way, we will make it.

# 13

# The Power of Love

*'Love never fails. But where there are prophecies,
they will cease; where there are tongues, they will be stilled;
where there is knowledge, it will pass away'*
I Corinthians 13:8.

We have reached the halfway mark of this wonderful, well-known chapter, 1 Corinthians 13, and as it happens, this phrase, 'Love never fails', is pivotal in this chapter. The scholars point out that it is at this stage that Paul shows why he has brought up this subject. What we have in the verse is a demonstration of the power of love. Power is something man has sought down through time. When asked, 'Why do you want to be president?' John F. Kennedy replied, 'Because that is where the power is.' Malcolm X said, 'Power never takes a back step, only in the face of more power.'

But how many have considered the power of love? One way of showing the abrupt, obvious contrast between Islam and Christianity is that Christianity centres on love; Islam – and as far as I know, they admit this – centres on hate. The question is, which is more powerful?

We are not thinking of sentimental love, or sexual love; we are talking about self-giving love, as Jesus described it in John 12:24:

'I tell you the truth, unless an ear of wheat falls to the ground and dies, it remains only a single seed. But if it dies, it produces many seeds. The man who loves his life will lose it, while the man who hates his life in this world will keep it for eternal life. Whoever serves me must follow me; and where I am, my servant also will be. My Father will honour the one who serves me.'

Graham Kendrick, in his song 'Meekness and Majesty' describes Jesus as 'Conquering through sacrifice'. This is what we mean by the power of love. It seems an absurdity, an incongruity – how *can* sacrifice result in power? But there is more power in self-giving love than in the whole of the universe, because it is God who is at work, who is determined to vindicate himself in his own way. Now this is because God is love. So we are talking about a demonstration of the power of God. Jesus said to the disciples, 'Do not leave Jerusalem but wait for the gift my Father promised ... You will receive power when the Holy Spirit comes on you' (Acts 1:3, 8). What we see operating on the day of Pentecost was the love of God filling these people. No-one had seen anything like it. And so the irony is, this power takes a step back! Love never fails.

One way of understanding what Paul means by love is to substitute 'Jesus' for the word. For example, in verse 4: Jesus is patient, Jesus is kind. Jesus does not envy, Jesus does not boast, Jesus is not proud. Jesus is not rude, Jesus is not self-seeking, Jesus is not easily angered, Jesus keeps no record of wrongs. And so in verse 8: Jesus never fails.

When I was a boy, back in the hills of Kentucky, we used to sing that old chorus: 'Jesus never fails. Heaven and earth may pass away, but Jesus never fails.' That doesn't mean that he wouldn't be persecuted or hated. After all, he died on a cross. Some called that failure. And so when we are talking about the power of love, it doesn't mean that we can use love to get what we want. Sadly, a lot of people try to use the church to get what they want, but that's not what we mean here by the power of love. To view this love as a gimmick that is going to get you from A to B and B to C is to miss the point that Paul is making here. We're talking about that which is God himself, and we can't use him. We can't manipulate God, we can't control God. This is not something that will enable us to get what we want, to achieve success. This is the curse of the 'Health and Wealth' gospel, the Prosperity gospel, the idea that if we are where we ought to be spiritually, will have money, or see miraculous things happen. That is not what the Bible teaches at all. We can't use God that way.

This *agape* love is non-manipulative, non-controlling. All of us by nature are manipulators, wanting to control people, treating them as objects, rather than human beings. We are all like this to a degree, because of our insecurity. The husband wants to control his wife; the wife wants to control her husband, and so on. But *agape* love is non-manipulative and is non-controlling. It is willing to be walked over, and go to the cross, and become powerless, that the power of God may flow.

**Paul's polemic**
The scholars tell us that this is not only a pivotal verse, but that it also begins the polemical section, where Paul is proving his point. Up to now he has been describing love, and it has been his goal, to 'sell' us on the idea of love, to convince us that it is the better way to live, the most excellent way. Some scholars claim that 1 Corinthians 13 was written by somebody else, that it was, perhaps, an early hymn and Paul included it for some reason. Others maintain that it was something he had been working on separately, and it seemed

appropriate to include it at this point. Both these theories are sheer nonsense, and the proof is this verse because Paul is showing that he has a general purpose, a general theme. And what was the purpose? To show that the *charismata* that attracted people then, and attract people now, are an inferior anointing compared to love.

There are two levels of anointing described in these verses, two kinds of power. On one level there is *charismata* – the ability to see miracles, wisdom, words of knowledge, healings, speaking in tongues, interpretation of tongues. But according to Paul, there is a higher level of anointing, *agape* love, and he is trying to make these Corinthians see that it is to be preferred. The question is, do we see that? Or are we more interested in that which will give us a feeling of power?

Now Paul is not putting down the *charismata* – he believes in them. In fact, in chapter 14 he comments: 'I speak in tongues more than all of you do.' And he has seen more miracles, signs and wonders than anybody else. So he is not putting down the *charismata*. What he is doing here is simply relativizing the gifts, putting them in perspective. These Corinthians, who thought they were so spiritual, had opted for the *charismata*, the grace-gifts. But Paul says there is a better way, and *agape* love is the superior, the supreme anointing. When he wrote to the church at Ephesus, he talked about Christ dwelling in us by faith (3:17). The person of Jesus, dwelling in us – that's the idea. And when that happens we will be a demonstration of the kind of person he was in the days of his flesh. There are a lot of ironies when it comes to this love. One irony is, we become powerless, so that the power of God may take over, but that means we have to wait for him to do it. And in the meantime we have to be nailed

to a cross and look like a fool, and be walked over and misunderstood. You ask, 'That's power?' We willingly lose the
battle to win the war. That's power. And Jesus will have the
last word. He that humbles himself shall be exalted; he that
exalts himself shall be abased.
    There are four things to consider from this verse.

**The priority of love**
Why is love to be preferred above the *charismata*? Because
Paul tells us, love never fails. The word translated 'fails'
comes from a word that means to fall. It is used in the Septuagint in 1 Samuel 3:19: 'The LORD was with Samuel and
he grew up and he let none of his words fall to the ground.'
This love will never be defeated, it will never be brought to
the ground. And so when we are being governed by love,
what we do, what we say, will be the way Jesus would have
done it, and the way Jesus would say it.
    So this is why love is preferable. However, it also means
this: the one who loves never falls. It is impossible to love
and to fall at the same time. Hebrews 6 talks about falling
away, but it is impossible to do that if we are living in love.
Love is the absolute guarantee that we will walk a straight
line. This is the way the writer of the epistle to the Hebrews
put it, 'Make level paths for your feet .... See to it that no-
one misses the grace of God and that no bitter root grows up
to cause trouble' (Heb. 12:13, 15). When we are governed
by love, it means that no root of bitterness will get us into
trouble and we will walk a straight line.
    Love never fails: what does this mean? For one thing it
means that love won't fail us. It won't let us down. Once
we have experienced it, even for a moment, we know why
Paul is trying to get these Corinthians to want it more than

the charismata. The reason it won't let us down is because it is the pure love of God, it is God. So it is when God takes over and when God is dwelling in our hearts like this. When Jesus Christ dwells in our hearts, we have the same sensitivity as the Holy Spirit. So on the one hand we say it is not really us and yet it is us. We stand apart from ourselves and say, 'I can't believe I've got this! I can't believe this is me!' We are amazed at it, it is as though we are spectators. And this is what God wants for all of us. It is the most wonderful thing in the world. Paul puts it like this in 1 Timothy 1:5: 'The goal of this command is love which comes from a pure heart and a good conscience and a sincere faith.' And then in 2 Timothy 1:7 he says: 'For God did not give us a spirit of timidity, but a spirit of power, of love and of self-discipline.' And so Paul could say in Ephesians 3:17: '... so that Christ may dwell in your hearts through faith. And I pray that you, being rooted and established in love, may have power ... to grasp how wide and long and high and deep is the love of Christ, and to know this love that surpasses knowledge – that you may be filled to the measure of all the fulness of God.' So, here is the first thing we learn from this verse: the priority of love.

**The permanence of love**
The second thing to learn from this verse is the permanence of love. There is some debate concerning this phrase. Should it be at the end of verse 7, which would read: 'Love always protects, always trusts, always hopes, always perseveres. Love never fails', or, is it a new statement, beginning verse 8: 'Love never fails: where there are prophecies they will cease, where there are tongues, they will be stilled'? If it is the former, it means that love is never defeated, if it is the latter,

it means that love never ends. All I can conclude is that it is both, it is the halfway mark in the chapter and it both sums up what has been said, and introduces a new section to show that love never comes to an end.

What does it mean, that love never comes to an end? First, it *doesn't* mean that those who once have experienced this love, will always experience it. I wish it were so. Once saved, always saved, that is true, but it is not true that once we have loved we will always love. It can leave us. For reasons I don't understand it lasts perhaps for only hours or days. When I first experienced it, it lasted for maybe six months. So, when it says it never ends it doesn't mean that once that love takes over we are set for life, because, for reasons I don't understand, we can experience it and lose it. One verse which, I think, proves this in Acts 23. When we read the Old Testament, we can see where Moses went wrong, or Joseph, and so on. Similarly, in the New Testament we find that Paul made mistakes, too. I don't mean by this that his epistles are fallible – they are infallible. In the book of Acts, Luke, writing under the same inspiration as Paul, describes at least two occasions where Paul was in the wrong. Acts 23:3, for example, was not Paul's finest hour. The high priest Ananias ordered those standing near Paul to strike him on the mouth, then Paul said to him, 'God will strike you, you whitewashed wall!' We might think, 'Oh well, if Paul said it, it must have been alright!' But I doubt he was filled with love at that moment. I think Luke records this incident to show that the great apostle Paul could have an unguarded moment. My point is that when Paul says love never fails or never ends, he doesn't mean that once we have had a taste of this love we are then set for life, because it is an anointing that we must guard very carefully. Notice he said earlier that love is not easily provoked – that is true, but it *can be provoked* and we can lose it.

So, what does this phrase mean? Partly this, the command to love is permanent. We are not commanded to have the charismata. They are not a sign of spirituality, but love is. It is a mark of unspirituality not to have love. Love is always going to be that which we are responsible for.

To put it another way, what he is saying is that the anointings of the charismata may actually come and go. Not only can love fade, but there comes a time when even the charismata won't be around. When the charismata are around they seem so right and natural we think they are going to be there for ever. But they are not something we can turn off and on, like a tap. If a person thinks this he doesn't have the real thing, because the real thing is like a well within that just comes – you can't turn it on. Now the point is that the anointing can go, but if it goes we are not to be regarded as less spiritual than before. But love is a permanent command. Love will always be a possibility and a responsibility. We can be rooted and established in love.

## The purpose of love

The third thing that we see from this verse is the purpose of love. What is love's aim? It is to take us where God wants us to go. The key is this; love doesn't flow with us, we flow with it. We can't use it to accomplish our own ends, but if we flow with it, we will accomplish what it aimed for. Just as Isaiah put it: 'So is my word that goes out from my mouth: It will not return to me empty, but will accomplish what I desire and achieve the purpose for which I sent it' (Isa. 55:11). When we go with love, we may find it takes us where we don't want to go. Perhaps love wants us to reach

out to a person who has hurt us, but we would rather judge
and criticize. If so, love disappears.

I can remember once, being picked up at the train station
to be taken to a conference where I was to speak. All the
way there the driver was saying, 'If only you'd been here
last night, the speaker was wonderful, they gave him a standing ovation. I'll get the tape for you.' Now, if I were really
spiritual, I would have said, 'Oh, I can hardly wait, this is
wonderful!' But instead I felt jealous and my pride was hurt.
That evening, that same speaker spoke again. I was sitting on
the platform near him as he spoke, right in the front where
everyone could see me. This time, however, his talk wasn't
so great, he 'got in the brush', as they would say in Kentucky.
He was floundering. For just a moment I was overjoyed – I do
hope it didn't show on my face. But suddenly, I felt so awful, I felt so convicted of my wrong response. And I began
to pray for that man. I knew he was in difficulty, and by
God's grace I began to intercede for him as though he were
my best friend, as though he were the one I had talked them
into getting, and as though I wanted him to excel. I found
myself standing apart from myself, wanting him to preach
with power. That wasn't me! Left to the flesh, I would have
wanted him to fail. But God is impartial, God wanted that
man to succeed as much as he wanted me to succeed the next
morning. God doesn't love me better than him. He was in
trouble and God said, Pray for him! This is the love we are
looking at. With this love, we go where it wants to take us.
We are not allowed to keep a record of a wrong, we are not
allowed to hold any kind of grudge.

To put it another way, love will make us treat others like
God treats us: graciously. God accepts us as we are, he forgets all our iniquities. The moment we refuse to flow with

love, however, we are in the flesh; we stick our feet in it, we become vindictive, we want our enemy to be exposed and punished.

The irony of this is that when love controls us, we won't be controlling. We will set the other person free because we are free. And so the purpose of love is just to feel with God; to rise above ourselves, and our personal concerns. God never fails and God is never frustrated. This is what Job learned at the end of his testing: 'I know that you can do all things; no plan of yours can be thwarted' (Job 42:2). The purpose of love is that we flow with God, and once we have tasted of this love we will prefer it a thousand times to any of the charismata. This is why Paul said: 'Do not be anxious about anything, but in everything, by prayer and petition, with thanksgiving, present your requests to God. And the peace of God, which transcends all understanding, will guard your hearts and your minds' (Phil. 4:6-7).

**The power of love**
Fourthly, the power of love is what it achieves. This is what God wanted us to achieve. We are just content with God's goal. Stephen demonstrated the immense power of love when he prayed for the people stoning him: 'Lord, do not hold this sin against them' (Acts 7:60). This is what God wanted – this display of love.

Stephen, who almost certainly was Paul's mentor, is one of the most outstanding people in all holy writ. I cannot express how much I admire him. I have wanted his anointing; 'they could not stand up against his wisdom or the Spirit by which he spoke' (Acts 6:10). 'All who were sitting in the Sanhedrin looked intently at Stephen, and they saw his face was like the face of an angel' (Acts 6:15). I have wished for that. And then I examine his mastery of the Old Testament (Acts 7) and observe how he put his opponents in the succession of the disobedient in ancient history – 'You are just like your fathers: You always resist the Holy Spirit!' (Acts 7:51). Although no one was immediately converted, never, never, never had one spoken with such power.

The whole time he spoke the pure love of God flowed through him and from him. The proof of this was his concern for them, not himself, when they were stoning him. He, therefore, fell on his knees and cried out, 'Lord, do not hold this sin against them.' It was a virtual re-enactment of Jesus' prayer on the cross, 'Father, forgive them, for they do not know what they are doing' (Luke 23:34).

The love of Christ that had indwelt Stephen got to Paul. That is partly why the risen Saviour said to Saul of Tarsus: 'It is hard for you to kick against the goads' (Acts 26:14). Paul wasn't able to shake off the power of love shown by Stephen. It led to the conversion of the greatest of the apostles.

Again, when Paul and Silas were in prison, they sang praises to God and love took over in extraordinary power. God affirmed them with such a violent earthquake that the foundations of the prison were shaken. Even the jailor was suddenly converted!

Malcolm X said, 'Power never takes a back step, only in the face of more power', but the power of love is that it does take a back step. The one who is filled with love allows the omnipotent God to move in. It becomes vulnerable, that is, the one governed by love is losing the battle to win the war. That's power.

# 14

# Opting for Excellence

'Love never fails. But where there are prophecies,
they will cease; where there are tongues, they will be stilled;
where there is knowledge, it will pass away'
1 Corinthians 13:8

Have you ever felt certain that there couldn't be anywhere better than where you are at that moment – your favourite restaurant, perhaps, or somewhere you have visited? But then you discover something else that so takes hold of you that you never return to your previous favourite. I am reminded of my maternal grandfather. He taught me to fish in Illinois. Our catches were never spectacular, but we loved to be out there, fishing. Years later, when I moved to Florida, I discovered salt-water fishing. I used to think of my grandfather; he just didn't know anything like bonefishing in the Florida Keys existed. It was completely beyond his experience. It made me see how a person can live in a little world and think that is all there is. It is this kind of comparison that the apostle Paul is wanting to make here. These people, because they spoke in tongues and saw certain things happening, thought this meant God was totally pleased with them. But they weren't nearly as spiritual as they thought and the truth is, Paul is now having to convince them of the idea of love being the most excellent way

## Why opt for excellence?
Why opt for excellence? Because, Paul says, 'where there are prophecies they will cease, where there are tongues, they

will be stilled, where there is knowledge, it will pass away.' There are certain minor difficulties with this passage. It has become a focal point for those who say that all Paul is talking about is that when the canon of Scripture is complete we will no longer need prophecies, words of knowledge, or tongues. These people claim to be persuaded in their hearts that there is no chance of charismata today, that it all ended in the earliest church. People who hold this view are called Cessationists. I don't know of many contemporary evangelical scholars who really hold that view. Most Cessationists are not thorough scholars and haven't really thought it through, because, as anyone can see, if that is what Paul was saying, these Corinthians wouldn't have had a clue what he meant. But they did know what he meant; they knew he wasn't talking about anything other than when the love of God comes, when we feel the love of the Father as Jesus felt it and passed it on to us, the love that casts out fear, then we have everything in perspective.

Now, when Paul says, 'Love never fails', he means that love will achieve its end, that we will never be exposed and embarrassed, when we do what we do in the love of the Holy Spirit. It means that love will accomplish God's purpose through us and it means that love will always be our responsibility. There is no 'Peter-principle' involved here. The Peter-principle is the idea that every person is promoted to the level of his incompetence. We are commanded to demonstrate the love of God, we are not commanded to have the charismata. And we are not to feel guilty if we don't speak in tongues or can't see a miracle, or don't know anything about words of knowledge, or prophecy. But we are commanded to love. Perhaps you are thinking, 'But that's beyond me, you don't know the bitterness I feel, and you don't know what they have done to me; you don't know the kind of father I had, you don't know the kind of mother I had, you don't know about this teacher who did this to me, you don't know about the kind of husband I've had to put up with, you don't realize what my son-in-law did, you don't realize what my boss did – if you did, you would feel angry too, and you would feel bitter too.' We need to realize that the command to love is not elevating us to the level of our incompetence. We can love, we can get rid of that bitterness, it does not have to stay there. What Paul is saying is that once we see what it will be like, when that bitterness is gone, then the charismata will be put into perspective.

The charismata have appeared on the scene at various stages throughout this century, and there have been times in church history when there was a touch of the unusual. But when they leave, they leave. There are those, however, who won't admit when they have gone, and many are unprepared to face life without them. And so Paul is warning the Corinthian Christians that the day is coming when this anointing with the charismata may just be lifted; there will be no word of knowledge, no prophecy, no speaking in tongues. What will we do then? We will still be commanded to love, and the only way to cope is if we learn to love. And so Paul is trying to persuade them of the best, the most excellent way. What amazes me is the way God graciously motivates us to do what we ought to have done anyway. God motivates us to become Christians, and God graciously shows us what we ought to do. And so with every believer. The obedience that he wants in us, motivates us, whether it is to a deeper level of consecration, or even something like tithing. God's motivation to give is: 'Bring the whole tithe into the storehouse ... and see if I will not throw open the floodgates of heaven and pour out so much blessing that you will not have room enough for it' (Mal. 3:10). Once we take him at his word and live this way over the years, we can see that God has been good to us to show us that.

In persuading us that the way of love is superior, Paul chooses three of the charismata from the list that he gave in 1 Corinthians 12:8-10: prophecy, tongues and word of knowledge. We know he is not against prophecy, because in chapter 14, he says that if we really desire a gift, this is the one we should want. The reason he mentions tongues, in all probability, is because so many believers then saw speaking in tongues as proof of spirituality. And people to this day tend to be just the same. Well, Paul is saying that that is not what spirituality is. People are misguided, then as now. But his purpose in mentioning these gifts is to compare the charismata with *agape* love.

The word that the NIV translates as 'cease' is the word *kartageo*. Its meaning is rather complex; it means 'cease', but it also means to render inactive, to remove from the sphere of activity or to be done away with. We come across this word a number of times in the New Testament. In Romans 3:3 it is translated as nullify. Paul says: 'What if some did not have faith? Will their lack of faith *nullify* God's faithfulness?' In Romans 6:6, it is translated as 'rendered powerless': 'For we know that our old self was crucified with him so that the body of sin might be *rendered powerless*.' In 1 Corinthians 2:6 it is translated as 'come to nothing': 'We do, however, speak a message of wisdom among the mature, but not the wisdom of this age or of the rulers of this age who, are *coming to nothing*.' So here are three ways to translate it – nullify, render powerless, come to nothing. So that is the word that is translated 'cease' here in 1 Corinthians 13:8. Where there are prophecies they will be rendered inactive, or put out of use, or be done away with, or set to one side.

So what does Paul mean? Is he taking for granted that prophecy will fail? The KJV says, 'Where there are prophecies they shall fail'. This is very misleading, however, because it implies that some prophecies just won't come true, and some prophecies don't. But the verse seems to give tacit approval of prophecies not coming true. But that's not the idea at all. Neither is he talking about the canon of Scripture being complete and thus making prophecies unnecessary.

## Love – perfect and continuing

The meaning is two things, both of which must be taken together, because one by itself will not give the complete picture. The first is to show by comparison that love is infinitely greater – the charismata will seem as nothing in comparison. Any gift that God gives us, he gives for the benefit of the whole body of Christ. But what happened in Corinth, and what often happens today, is that we seek a gift not because of what it will do for the body, but for what it will do for us, and that is completely wrong. We have got to ask the question, 'Why do I want the charismata?' And the truth is, our motivation is selfish. I have had to ask myself this question, time and time again, 'Why do I want to preach well?' Is it so people will say, 'Very good!' Or is it that I want to be a blessing to those who hear me? And so, we must ask these kinds of questions when it comes to any gift. Is it really to be a blessing to others, or is it so that we will have our egos inflated?

What Paul is showing here is that when the perfect comes along, the charismata by comparison seem as nothing. And so it is far better that we are rooted and grounded in love.

The second meaning is that the command to love will always be our responsibility. We ought to be grateful for any appearance of the charismata for they are a sign of the anointing, a type of genuine revival. When George Whitefield preached there was a great demonstration of the Spirit and many were struck unconscious. Similarly in America with the preaching of Edwards, and in the Cane Ridge revival in Kentucky. There was a touch of it in Wales in 1904-1905 when unusual things happened at the time. But when this anointing lifted, many people went into deep depression because they didn't see the unusual happening all the time. What Paul is pointing out is that prophecies will one day cease, but the command to love remains, and what will enable us to cope in the absence of the charismata is this love.

## The imperfections of the charismata

The charismata, by their very nature, are imperfect in themselves. I want to point out five things the charismata have in common.

First, they are inflating. They inflate the ego, they will exalt you: 'Knowledge puffeth up' says 1 Corinthians 8:2 (KJV). The person who has the gift of prophecy will be vulnerable to the temptation of pride. But love is self-effacing and focuses upon the well-being of others.

Second, the charismata are intimidating: they make other people stand in awe of you. Any extraordinary gift will make others feel inferior. I know of a preacher whose gift is so great that when I hear him preach I get depressed. I wish I could preach like him! But Jesus never intimidated. That is the thing about love; it never intimidates, it puts people at ease. The more you are filled with love, the more people swarm round you. And there was something about the person of Jesus that made any tramp, or beggar, or sinner feel, 'If I can just get to him, I know he will accept me.' That's love, but a gift can be intimidating.

Third, the charismata are isolated from the fruit of the Spirit. This is why having a gift of the Spirit will not make you spiritual. As we have already seen, you can speak in tongues and not be spiritual, and so on. Because the gifts and calling of God are irrevocable, the truth is that we can have the charismata and not be living a godly life. I remember hearing a sermon that I thought was one of the greatest sermons I had ever heard. Two years later, however, I found out that at that time the preacher's personal life was far from godly; he was having an affair with someone in his church. How could he preach a sermon like that and yet live like that? We can have the charismata, which can be the gift of preaching or speaking in tongues, and not be spiritual.

Fourth, the charismata are insatiable. If a person is given a prophecy, thrilling though it may be, in a few weeks' time he will want just a little bit more and then a little bit more, and so on. I know of people who have the gift of knowledge, who, when they give a word to somebody, are then given no peace, because the person wants to know more and more. No matter what the gift is, it won't completely satisfy, we will always want just another bit more. Whereas love completely satisfies.

Fifth, the charismata are intermittent. They come and they go, but Jesus says, concerning love, 'If you obey my commands you will remain in my love' (John 15:10). Prophecies will cease, tongues will be stilled. This comes from a Greek word, *posante*, that means to cease, to stop, to subside. Paul is not running down the gift of tongues, but he says they will be stilled. We can't speak in tongues all the time, but we can always love.

Similarly, 'where there is knowledge, it will *pass away*' (this is the same word *kartageo* that earlier in the verse is translated 'cease'). The different translation is just for variety. Knowledge will 'pass away', it always does. The immediate effect of a word of knowledge is to give a good feeling, but eventually it will pass away.

## Love – greater by far

Any kind of gift helps us, but what would be far better is if each of us could for ourselves experience this love of God that casts out fear, that destroys the desire to have anybody punished or hurt or exposed. Paul says this is the most excellent way.

Think of the passage in John 13:37-38 where Peter asked. 'Lord, why can't I follow you now? I will lay down my life for you.' Jesus replied, 'Will you really lay down your life for me? I tell you the truth, before the cock crows, you will disown me three times.' Then, turning to all the disciples he says, 'Do not let your hearts be troubled' (John 14:1). In the original, there were no chapters and verses, or full stops. Jesus is talking to the whole group: 'You will disown me three times, don't let your hearts be troubled, you believe in God.'

What can we learn from this? When Jesus appeared in the upper room after his resurrection and said to the eleven disciples: 'Peace', that meant far more than when he had walked on water, or fed the five thousand. The love they felt from Jesus meant a thousand times more than all the miracles they had ever witnessed. The charismata is supposed to do something for the body, but most who seek the gifts want them for themselves. But with the love of God we can have it both ways: to live without fear, to live without guilt, to live without the need to prove ourselves. Paul is trying to help the Corinthians choose excellence. He is wanting to convince them that there is something better than prophecy, or words of knowledge, or signs and wonders: the love of God. Were this love to grip us and were we to live by it, that would dazzle the world.

# 15

# Perfect Love

*'For we know in part and we prophesy in part, but
when perfection comes, the imperfect disappears'*
I Corinthians 13:9-10

These words, 'when perfection comes, the imperfect disappears,' form a general principle that stands on its own and could be applied to a thousand situations. So we need to ask why this statement is included and what the whole of verse 10 means.

What does Paul mean by perfection, the perfect that is to come? Two things; first, what is available to us now – namely, a preview of perfection, and secondly, what we will have throughout eternity if we are saved – namely, perfect love. What Paul means by 'perfection' is what one Puritan referred to as 'heaven on earth'. God offers Christians a little bit of heaven on the way to heaven. What worries me, more than anything, is that this love which is available, I fear is the least experienced of anything. It is important that we understand this verse, but more particularly that we get a taste of this 'heaven on earth' for ourselves.

## A preview of perfection
This is a preview of things to come. When Paul talks about that which is perfect, he is speaking eschatologically. Eschatology refers to the last times, the end, the future, when Jesus comes. The Greek word is *eschaton*. The book of Revelation is an

eschatological preview. When we read the book of Revelation, we get a preview of things to come. And God, once in a while, does this in the present. What I mean is that sometimes we get a taste of what will take place one day, when Jesus returns. Revival, really, is a little bit of heaven on earth, or a little bit of the judgment seat of Christ brought forward, so that when revival comes, it exposes where we are spiritually. When Ananias and Sapphira lied to the Holy Spirit and were then struck dead, that was really the *eschaton*, the judgment, just brought forward. When a person is healed, it is really the eschaton brought forward, because one day all believers will be healed, and there will be no sickness or pain. So, an eschatological preview is when we get a taste of things to come.

God also does this with regard to his own love. The day is coming when we will dwell in God and will know his love and will know it throughout eternity. There will be no fear, there will be perfect love towards each other, there will be no uneasiness with anybody; there won't be one part of heaven where you can't go because they aren't speaking to you at the present time. Everybody is going to love everybody. It will be perfect in that way. But sometimes we get an eschatological preview; God brings forward this perfection. John calls it perfect love (1 John 4:18), and that is what Paul means: when that which is perfect comes, that which is imperfect will be done away with.

## Perfection for eternity

The second meaning is that gifts will cease entirely because no prophecies will be needed in heaven, there will be no praying in tongues for intercession, or in order to show the unbeliever what God can do through an unknown tongue. There will be no need for words of knowledge, for one day the gifts will cease. And so this verse refers to what can happen in the here and now when the love of God comes: the gifts are upstaged by love, but then in the eschaton, when we are glorified, the gifts will cease for ever.

In the previous chapter we noted that this is not a reference to the gifts ceasing long ago by God's design. Rather, this verse is showing first, that when the love of God is experienced and the eschaton is brought forward, and we feel that love, all of the charismata are put in perspective, eclipsed by this love. But then, secondly, it refers to the final eschaton when the charismata will be rendered obsolete by the coming of Jesus.

Between verses 8 and 10 is this phrase: 'For we know in part and we prophesy in part'. This is the reason that verse 8 is true: 'Where there are prophecies they will cease; where there are tongues, they will be stilled; where there is knowledge, it will pass away. For we know in part ....' These things will pass away because the charismata are destined to oblivion, being imperfect to begin with. In verse 9 Paul mentions only two of the charismata – word of knowledge and prophecy. He could have referred to nine or ten of the charismata, but he singled out these two because they are so limited. A person with an extraordinary prophetic gift doesn't see everything, he knows only in part. He may just have a little word with someone and that word will be spot on and transform their lives, and others will think, 'Oh, he knows everything!' But he doesn't, he just knows a little bit.

So what exactly does Paul mean by this word, 'perfect'?

## The parallel of love
There are two sorts of power in God's economy and they are parallel. Imagine travelling down a road and coming to

a place where it forks. You have got to decide whether to turn right or turn left, but both roads are going in the same direction. They are parallel to each other. Both roads show two ways of going forward. Well, imagine this now with regard to your Christian pilgrimage: you come to a point where you have to decide whether you want to turn right, or turn left, but the two roads are parallel. One road is the charismata, and if you take that road you can experience the gift of healing, miracles, word of knowledge, discerning of spirits, speaking in tongues. The other road, however, is the way of brokenness, meekness, honesty, humility, the pure love of God. And so the question is, when you come to that place, would you like to go the charismatic route, or would you like to go down the pure-love-of-God route. And so what Paul is doing here is showing the parallel of love and he is asking the Corinthians to choose which road they want. Most people, it would seem, want the power that emanates from the gifts. That is understandable. Wouldn't it be wonderful if the eschaton could be brought forward and people were healed, and miracles occurred in the way they did in the earliest church? Well, the church at Corinth were experiencing a lot of that. But the apostle Paul tells them there is a parallel route and it is better. Alongside the charismata there is something else, and it is the most excellent way.

## The possibility of love

Why do we have this chapter in 1 Corinthians? Why does Paul tell us about the nature of *agape* love? Is he simply dangling a carrot in front of us that we will never get a hold of? Are we to believe that Paul is trying to convince us of something that ultimately is unobtainable, unachievable? Is this most excellent way the most unlikely way? Or could it be that it is a way that is available to us, this side of heaven? Paul's intention is to show us the possibility of love.

Remember, the love in question is the pure love of God, the unhindered, ungrieved Holy Spirit shedding love in our hearts. Think again of Stephen, when he stood before the Council, we are told his face shone like an angel. And he was able to speak in such a way that no-one could resist his wisdom. Then at the end of his defence when they began to stone him, he spoke his last words: 'Lord, do not hold this sin against them.'

Have you ever prayed that the very one who has mistreated you most would be totally forgiven by God and his sin not even be remembered? Is it not rather the case that when some-one hurt us, we want God to deal with them? That is the most natural reaction, and we can mistake it for a spiritual reaction, after all, doesn't the Bible say, 'Vengeance is mine'? So we just say, 'Lord, you deal with so-and-so, for doing what he did.' But if anyone had cause to pray this, it was Stephen, yet he prayed, 'Lord, do not hold this sin against them.'

Did he have unusual grace, just because he was getting ready to go to heaven? A lot of the old saints, particularly the old Presbyterians and the early Methodists, talked about 'dying grace', where a dying person would experience the glory of the Lord filling the room and be aware of an over-whelming sense of the love of God. But some of them were healed and lived for many years. And they knew that this love was a possibility and wasn't just for dying. And that is why some of the saints in history have experienced this, and that is why Paul not only shows us the parallel of love, the charismata, but says that love is the better way; he is showing us the possibility of love.

## The perfection of love

When Paul writes, 'When that which is *perfect* ...', the word
he uses is the same as the one used by John when he wrote:
'There is no fear in love. But *perfect* love drives out fear,
because fear has to do with punishment. The man who fears
is not made perfect in love' (1 John 4:18). And so here is that
eschatological preview, the last day brought forward, when
we are given a taste of the kind of love we are going to have
throughout eternity. Paul is *not* talking about the perfection
of a Christian. That is what happens when we are glorified:
'... those whom he predestined, he also called; those whom
he called, he also justified; those whom he justified, he also
glorified' (Rom. 8:30) – we shall be like Jesus, we shall see
him as he is. So Paul is not talking about the perfection of a
Christian, but about the love that enables the Christian *not
to fear*.

There is a difference between fearlessness and courage.
Courage is the strength to do something in the face of fear.
Fearlessness, however, is the total absence of fear. John
talks about having this fearlessness on the day of judgment.
Whereas there will be those weeping and gnashing their
teeth from fear, John talks of the believer having boldness
in the day of judgment; it will be the most glorious moment
we have ever known. And Paul is saying that we can have a
little bit of that right here.

If this glimpse of love we are given now is only in measure, how can it be called perfect? I answer: If you were to go
to the ocean and dip a glass into the water, you would then
have a glass of water that is taken from the ocean and what
is in it is the pure ocean. In quantity it is nothing compared
to the vastness of the ocean, but everything that is true of
the ocean is there. And so, the perfection that both Paul and

John are talking about is a taste of the pure love of God. It doesn't make us perfect, but it enables us to experience, that is, taste perfect love.

Perfect love is characterized by the absence of certain things. For example, there is an absence of rudeness. Paul, in an earlier verse, said, 'Love is not rude.' It is also characterised by an absence of ridicule. How easy it can be to make another person look ridiculous. But perfect love drives out fear that is characterized by the need to make others look ridiculous. And when fear is driven out, there is an absence of rudeness, of ridicule, and of rift. Nobody with this love will want to disrupt the unity. If two people have this love then there will be no rift between them. If two dozen people have this love, it would be most extraordinary. In the earliest church, when there was so much love, they all had everything in common, they just didn't care about their property, it didn't mean a thing to them. Some think it went too far, and there is perhaps some merit in that view, but the question is, why did they want to do it? They had a taste of heaven on earth, and they were detached from any kind of rivalry. The spirit of jealousy was totally gone; there was no sense of the need to compete or prove themselves.

Perfect love is also characterized by an absence of resentment. Resentment, like ridicule and rivalry, is based on fear. When someone has insulted you or hurt you, you naturally feel resentful. But the love of God evaporates resentment like the sun evaporates mist.

When the pure love of God emerges in the heart there is an absence of regret, and this is remarkable. Without love we all have our regrets. Without love we all have guilt problems. We say, 'If only ...' But when the pure love of God dwells in the heart, we are at peace with ourselves, at peace with the past and the present. The promise of Romans 8:28 is very real, 'All things work together for good' and similarly, Joel 2:25, 'I will repay you for the years that the locusts have eaten.' We can know with certainty that every-thing is going to work together for good, for the pure love of God takes away regret because you know God is going to put it right. This is a foretaste of heaven. In heaven there will be no regrets, there will be no tears, there will be no pain.

It is an absence of revenge. John said, 'fear has to do with punishment'. The need to punish someone is because you are afraid; therefore, when perfect love drives out fear, the need for revenge is gone. The desire for vindication disappears also. In fact, we become repulsed by the thought that we once felt we deserved to be vindicated. We experience what Isaiah felt when he saw the pure holiness of God, described in Isaiah 6. The Seraphim cried, 'Holy, holy, holy is the LORD of hosts!' And Isaiah felt awful, and said, 'Woe is me! I am undone!' But without seeing the holiness of God, we feel that we deserve vindication, we want our rights. Sin is so blinding that we never see our own sin in the same light as the sin of others. But when the pure love of God emerges, there is a total absence of the need to have revenge.

Perfect love is also characterized by the absence of rage. 'Let all bitterness and rage and malice cease from you,' writes Paul in Ephesians 4:31. And in 1 Corinthians 13:5 he writes: 'Love is not easily angered'. The pure love of God overlooks that which normally makes us annoyed and irritable. It is wisdom to overlook a matter.

When the pure love of God emerges in the heart, our world is turned upside down. There will be no grudging, no envy, no lust, no need to be seen or to be recognized. It is more wonderful than fulfilled ambition, more wonderful than the adulation of thousands. As Brother Lawrence put it in his book, *The Practice of the Presence of God*, he would just as soon pick up a straw from the ground as preach to thousands. The pure love of God just wants the Father's glory.

But what happens when our experience of this love fades? When it fades, envy returns, fear returns, panic returns, the need to prove ourselves returns, lurking charismata become so much more important. So, we may well ask, what's the use of having it if it is going to fade? Answer: it is to let us know what to pray for, this most excellent way. We become aware that we are sinning. Prior to experiencing this perfect love we may not even have recognized our own sin, but love produces a keener sense of sin.

For those who choose the route of the perfection of love instead of the charismata they may find they get both! Choose the route of the gifts, and love almost certainly will be absent. Choose the route of perfect love and do not be surprised if the charismata emerge stronger than ever! The principle – 'He who saves his life will lose it, he who loses it will find it' – is at stake here.

One day the perfect will come; at the last day, when we are glorified, there will be no fading away. But the rediscovery of the pure love of God, by personal encounter, by personal experience, is to be sought above all else. There is nothing else like it, even if it fades away, because after it fades away, having had a taste of it, we know what our responsibility is. And so this love is a possibility, we must want it more than anything else in the world. God is a jealous God and he will not allow any rivals. But to those who crave this most excellent way God will give this most excellent spirit, and we will begin to experience what the saints of old had known. It is a possibility, and may God hasten the day.

# 16

## Growing Up

'When I was a child, I talked like a child, I thought like a child,
I reasoned like a child. When I became a man,
I put childish ways behind me'
I Corinthians 13:11

We are getting near to the end of this great chapter of the New Testament, commonly called 'The Love Chapter.' The verse in question here is possibly one of the best-known verses in the chapter. 'When I was a child, I talked like a child, I thought like a child, I reasoned like a child. When I became a man, I put childish ways behind me'.

This verse stands on its own, and we all know exactly what it means. The question is why did Paul put it here? May I remind you that it is in the context of Paul seeking to motivate us to aspire after the love of God in our hearts more than anything in the world. He is trying to show us that the transition from walking in the flesh to walking in the Spirit is going to be painful, but that we do need to make the transition, it is only a matter of time. He is saying, in effect, 'Grow up!' It is always embarrassing to be told, 'You are being childish!' But we all are, from time to time, for there is a little child in all of us, and none of us is perfectly mature, only Jesus Christ of Nazareth was the perfect Man. On the other hand, we ought to feel ashamed of any childish behaviour, and Paul wants us to make the transition to maturity. There are those who take the view that Paul here is talking of glorification, of making the transition from this life to the next. But I don't think that is what it means, for two reasons. First of all, when we make the transition to heaven it will be a crisis, we will be glorified in the twinkling of an eye. But this verse does not describe a crisis, but a process.

Secondly, the main reason we know he is not talking about glorification is that Paul's whole object is to help these Corinthians come to want love more than anything in the world. Since Paul is talking about love it stands to reason that what he is doing here is comparing Christians without love to weak and childish babes in Christ, and hoping that they will come to maturity and manhood. This, without question, is a throwback to an earlier passage in the epistle, where he accuses these Corinthians of being childish: 'I could not address you as spiritual, but as worldly – mere infants in Christ. I gave you milk, not solid food, for you were not ready for it. Indeed, you are still not ready. You are still worldly ... there is jealousy and quarrelling among you, are you not worldly?' (1 Cor. 3:1). Their childish lifestyle has already been commented on.

Now when Paul uses this word, 'child', it is the same word he uses in Ephesians 4:14: 'Then we will no longer be *infants*, tossed back and forth by the waves, and blown here and there by every wind of teaching ...'. It is the word used by the writer of Hebrews: 'though by this time you ought to be teachers, you need someone to teach you the elementary truths of God's word all over again. You need milk, not solid food! Anyone who lives on milk, being still an *infant*, is not acquainted with the teaching about righteousness' (Heb. 5:12-13). The Christian who has not learned to love is compared to a child. And, that is what a child is. A child is one who has to be loved; the mature person is the one who sees the need to *be loving*.

Now Paul is not calling the charismata childishness. Some have interpreted this passage in this way, but Paul is not saying that at all. He affirms the gifts and we should affirm the gifts. What is childish is to think that that is spirituality. The childishness is saying that because we have the gifts, we are spiritual. But we can have these gifts and not have love. The childishness is saying that these gifts are everything. The most excellent way is the way of love; maturity is choosing the most excellent way.

Is Paul speaking autobiographically when he says, 'When I was a child ...'? Is he referring to himself, or is it just an illustration? Well, the answer is both. He certainly uses it as an illustration, but I don't think he could have talked like this if he himself had not been brought through the painful process of having to grow up. Paul was once a babe in Christ, but he needed to grow up. Have you noticed that there are two careers in the life of Paul? The first was right after he was converted. In no time he was out on the streets witnessing and talking about Jesus (Acts 9). But then we don't hear of Paul for a while. Where did he go? In Galatians 1 and 2 he fills in the blanks for us, recounting how God took him to Arabia and then to Damascus, and how he was seen by virtually nobody for fourteen years. You can mark it down that those were the years when Paul became a man.

Now, is this verse in any way a contradiction of Jesus' words: 'I tell you the truth, anyone who will not receive the kingdom of God like a little child will never enter it' (Mark 10:15)? Superficially it may appear to be a contradiction because Jesus says we must be like a child, but Paul says we must put childish ways behind us. What Jesus calls for is that we be open and willing to be taught like a child, and not know it all. In that sense, we all need to climb down. But what Paul describes as childishness is that which persists longer than it should. And humanly speaking, some do mature faster than others. In psychology there is what is called arrested development, where a person seems to stay at a certain emotional age, even though he is advanced in years. There are a number of reasons for this. Freud has said that too little or too much gratification at any particular age can fix a person at that age. A trauma at the age of five, for example, sometimes leaves a person with the emotional age of five for a long time, and some never come out of it. The point is we can have arrested emotional development even though we are advanced in years.

Childishness is demonstrated in certain ways. A child doesn't listen to reason: 'When I was a child, I reasoned as a child.' A child demands instant gratification, is unaware of danger; lacks discernment; is totally preoccupied with him or herself. And so this verse is an implicit rebuke to these carnal Christians of Corinth. Paul is telling them, 'Grow up, not just emotionally, but spiritually.' And yet, at the natural level, we all resist growing up. By nature we are congenitally opposed to change. Any opposition to change isn't a sign of being spiritual. This is the way we all are. The trauma of birth, psychologists tell us, is the greatest trauma we have ever gone through. When we were born, we didn't want to leave our mother's womb. Then there is the trauma of being weaned as a child, the trauma of going to school. I can remember the spot on the road, in Ashland, Kentucky, where I was when my parents told me I would be starting school the following week. I was six years old, and I was horrified. I don't know that they hadn't told me before then – they probably did, but for some reason, the penny dropped and I realized that I was going to have to go to school and be with other kids and I was terrified. We all want to stay young, and some, perhaps more than others, want to look young and find it painful to grow old and to look old. But, at the spiritual level, the same thing is true; after conversion there are those who want to hang on a bit to what they were converted from. And this is why James says to them:

> What causes fights and quarrels among you? Don't they come from your desires that battle within you? You want something but don't get it. You quarrel and fight ... you adulterous people, don't you know that friendship with the world is hatred towards God? Anyone who chooses to be a friend of the world becomes an enemy of God (James 4:1, 2, 4).

When a person has become a Christian and has known sweet fellowship with God but then looks back in regret at his previous life, feeling a little sorry for himself that he is not enjoying something that he used to enjoy, in that moment, God takes notice and he becomes like an enemy. Whoever chooses to be a friend of the world becomes an enemy of God. And so at the spiritual level we resist being changed from glory to glory, but walking in the light leads to love and maturity. Refusing to walk in the light will keep us in selfishness and immaturity.

There are three stages in this verse: the childhood stage, the manhood stage, and the painful process in between.

## A painless pursuit

Childhood could well be described as a painless pursuit. We expect children to behave in certain ways, to talk, think and reason like a child. We all recognize the sound of a child. I remember once meeting a beautiful seventeen-year-old. If you didn't look at her, however, and simply heard her voice, you would have said she was probably 8 or 9 years old. I couldn't get over it. It appeared that her parents didn't want her to grow up, and talked to her as if she were still a little child. Consequently she sounded like a little girl, in order to please them. Similarly, we can listen to people talk, who have been Christians for years, and think, 'I don't believe this! This is a Christian of longstanding and talking like that!' Immature speech in people who have been Christians for many years is to their shame, and Paul is challenging the believers over this.

The painless pursuit of childhood is marked by a particular way of talking and also a particular way of thinking; 'I thought as a child', said Paul. A child is the most selfish person that ever was. For the whole world centres on him, as far as he is concerned. He thinks only of himself, and wants immediate gratification. He wants to be loved, but it never crosses his mind to be loving. And some of us, who have been Christians for quite some time, have never moved beyond just wanting to be loved, pampered and encouraged. When will we take the responsibility and begin to grow up? If we are still waiting for others to show if they care about us, we need to start caring instead.

A third characteristic of children is shallowness. A child is easily influenced, is gullible, and has no discernment. This gullibility is why we have to say to a child, 'Don't talk to strangers.' And this is why Paul says we should no longer be infants who are tossed about by every wind of doctrine. Certain cults like to fish in the Christian pond, such as Jehovah's Witnesses or the Church of Christ, or the Mormons, because they have found that spiritual infants are an easy catch. These infants, who are gullible, don't know what they believe, and are easily influenced. They are shallow like a child. This point is expanded more fully in the second letter to the Corinthians, where Paul says:

> I am afraid that just as Eve was deceived by the serpent's cunning, your minds may somehow be led astray from your sincere and pure devotion to Christ. For if someone comes to you and preaches a Jesus other than the Jesus we preached, or if you receive a different spirit from the one you received, or a different gospel from the one you accepted, you put up with it easily enough (2 Cor. 11:3, 4).

So immaturity in Christians is just like the painless pursuit of childhood, characterized by baby-talk, selfishness and shallowness.

## A painful process
The second of the three stages referred to is the painful transition from childhood to maturity: 'When I became a man.' Nobody said it would be easy. You can become a man physically by time alone: you come to puberty, and there are physical changes, and that is just because of the years. But that isn't what Paul means and that isn't the way it happens spiritually; it takes more than just the passing of time to produce maturity. Spiritual maturity, spiritual manhood, doesn't come automatically. It comes as a result of a painful process.

This painful process involves three things: resisting temptation; responding positively to trial; and recognizing and resisting the devil. Temptation comes in many forms, usually in one of three categories – money, sex or power. Anyone facing responsibilities in the church of God has got to prove that he or she can be trusted not to yield to sexual temptation. Perhaps some are not where they should be today, because they failed the test.

Joseph proved himself in this area. He was earmarked to be Prime Minister of Egypt, but he had to be tested first and one of the tests was to see how he responded to sexual temptation.

If we are going to become mature, we have got to learn to resist. I didn't say it would be easy. It is a painful process, it hurts. We must resist sex outside of marriage; that includes pre-marital sex, extra-marital sex or homosexual activity. Some men feel the need to prove their manhood by flirting with younger women; but that's not being a man. Being a man is standing tall and saying, 'No.' Resisting sexual temptation is a mark of maturity.

Another area where temptation comes in is money. 'The love of money is a root of all kinds of evil. Some people, eager for money, have wandered from the faith,' says Paul, 'and pierced themselves with many griefs' (1 Tim. 6:10). Some haven't learned to handle money, and maybe that is the reason why God doesn't always give us what we want at a financial level; he knows what we will do with the money as soon as we get it. Perhaps we think misguidedly that love of money only applies to those who want to drive a Rolls Royce or a Jaguar. But greed takes many forms, some grand and others not so grand. Basically, it is craving to satisfy our appetite. Learning to handle money is part of this painful maturing process.

The third area of temptation is to have power. It is the temptation to be in control – to control people, to manipulate. It is the temptation to be seen as 'top dog', to be above others, so we can look down on them. It stems from the need to feel important, to be admired. It also emerges from personal insecurity, where our self-esteem is that where our ego is so fragile that the slightest thing ticks us off and no-one can get

near us, and we are full of bitterness and holding the grudge.
We can't stand the humbling job or someone saying anything
about us that is not very pleasant. Childish. And it could be
that many of us could be so much further along than we are.
We aspire to the same things that the world aspires to, and
we get our feelings hurt just like the world.

So, the painful process to maturity involves learning to
resist temptation, but it also involves responding positively
to trial. When we experience bereavement, financial reverse,
sickness, pain, it may be a test to see whether we are going
to put God first. On-going loneliness, or a sudden change
of lifestyle, or a difficult relationship at work are all tests
to see whether we want love more than anything. How we
cope with difficulty shows whether we have passed the test
of maturity. If we react bitterly, saying, 'Well, I prayed and
God didn't help me,' we are still immature. The mark of
maturity is when we have learned to look at our trials and
say, like Job, 'Though he slay me, yet will I hope in him'
(Job 13:15).

The third part of this painful process is learning to recognize and resist the devil. The devil is Jesus Christ's arch-
enemy and we show our love for Jesus by resisting the devil.
When we resist, he will flee from us. Now the point is, God
uses these things to bring us to manhood. It will not come
by simply raising our hand at the end of the church service
and saying, 'I want to walk closer to God.' Instead, it will
come on Tuesday afternoon, or next Wednesday afternoon,
or next Friday, when we are in the heat of the battle! What
we are like when we are by ourselves, this is when we become mature. It is a painful process, but God will do things
to get your attention, to enforce the learning, to bring us to
maturity. It is a painful process.

## A past performance

'When I became a man, I put childish ways behind me.'
Why past performance? Well, in the Greek it is the perfect
tense and it means that he put away childish things by decision and with finality. It is the strongest tense in the Greek
language. In other words, it is done, it is not a question of
looking over your shoulder and seeing how close you can
get to the world and still say, 'No.' As Paul put it in his letter to Titus: 'For the grace of God that brings salvation has
appeared to all men. It teaches us to say "No" to ungodliness
and worldly passions, and to live self-controlled, upright and
godly lives in this present age, while we wait for the blessed
hope – the glorious appearing of our great God and Saviour,
Jesus Christ' (Titus 2:11-13).

These things are put irrevocably behind us. Money, sex,
power, are under control, and dealt with. It doesn't mean we
won't be tempted, but according to James, we are responsible
for our own temptations. Temptation is not a sin, but we are
responsible for our temptation because James said, 'When
tempted, no-one should say, "God is tempting me." For God
cannot be tempted by evil, nor does he tempt anyone; but each
one is tempted when, by *his own evil desire*, he is dragged
away and enticed' (James 1:13-14). Playing the man is not
easy, but we must do it. In Broad Street in Oxford there is a
cross in the road that marks the spot where, in 1555, Bishop
Hugh Latimer, 70 years old, and Bishop Nicholas Ridley,
40 years old, were burned to death for treason. They were
tied back to back and, as the fire was lit, the aged Latimer
shouted to Ridley, 'Fear not, Master Ridley, and play the man!
We shall this day light such a candle in England, that I trust
shall never be put out!' How can we play the man? We do
so when, by God's grace, we resist temptation, and react to

the trial in a way that brings dignity and honour to God. The day will come when the great test will be presented and we will pass it as well. 'He that is faithful in that which is least is faithful also in much' (Luke 16:10, KJV).

# 17

# When God Tells Us Why

'Now we see but a poor reflection as in a mirror;
then we shall see face to face. Now I know in part;
then I shall know fully, even as I am fully known'
I Corinthians 13:12

We are coming to the end of this glorious chapter, this is the penultimate verse. It is a very wonderful verse; the more I think about it, the more I wonder what we would do without it. All my life I have believed that one day we shall have all of our questions answered; one day God will explain things to us and tell us why. But, do we have any evidence for this in the Bible? Well, according to this verse, one day God will tell us why. One day. But when will that be? It will not be immediately after we die. There is what is called the intermediate state, the time between our deaths and the second coming of Jesus. In Revelation 6:9, John describes how he saw the souls under the altar who had been slain for the Word of God, and they were crying out, 'How long, Sovereign Lord, holy and true, until you judge the inhabitants of the earth and avenge our blood?' So although these *souls* (not physical bodies) were in heaven, they still didn't have that question answered. They wondered, 'How long?'

So when the apostle Paul says that one day 'I shall know fully, even as I am fully known,' he is not talking about knowledge that becomes ours at the moment of death. It is wrong to assume that people in heaven understand everything now. Revelation 6:9-10 shows that is not the case. But we do know that one day, when Jesus comes the second time, on that Day of days God will clear his name. That will be the beginning of the era that will never end, and God will tell us why.

So once again we are looking here at an eschatological verse. Paul is referring to the eschaton, the Day of days, when Jesus will return and we will be glorified. That is Paul's word, we will be *glorified* (Rom. 8:30).

Verse 12 links back to verses 9 and 10, which read, 'For we know in part and we prophesy in part, but when perfection comes, the imperfect disappears.' Those verses refer to two things: first, an eschatological preview of God's own love – the perfection that makes everything else insignificant; and secondly, eschatological perfection, 'when that which is perfect is come,' when we are glorified.

The second reason that Paul brings in this verse is in keeping with his general purpose. We have noted on a number of occasions in this book that 1 Corinthians 13 is not Paul's attempt to write a beautiful chapter on love. We may call it the 'Love Chapter' of the Bible, but this is only part of a general point he is making. He is showing us the most excellent way. He wanted to show that the pure love of God is better than the charismata. The Corinthian believers thought the gifts of the Spirit were the most important thing in the world, the mark of true spirituality. But Paul says they don't prove anything. Whereas love is the most excellent way. There is nothing greater than the pure love of God being our motivation for everything we do. They had maximised the importance of the gifts and the idea of love, sadly, hardly crossed their minds.

So, why bring in eschatology at all? The answer to that is that the charismata, the gifts of the Spirit, at best leave our questions unanswered. Paul is showing us that we need to look beyond. When he writes: 'Now we see but a poor reflection as in a mirror', he means that even if we have the gift of prophecy, or word of knowledge, at best, we see but a poor reflection of the real thing. But then he says, one day all our questions will be answered, so don't try to understand everything now.

Apart from the eschatological implications, this verse is a rebuke to those who claim to have 'arrived'. Sadly, some would not admit to seeing but a poor reflection. They claim to know more. One well-known Health and Wealth preacher from America is on record as saying: 'If the apostle Paul had my faith, he would not have had his thorn in the flesh.' Think about that. There are those who think they have moved beyond the apostle Paul, beyond the New Testament. And there are those who feel they must have all the answers, and go further into theology and philosophy and education, needing to prove they are learned. The apostle Paul, however, admits he doesn't have all the answers: 'Now we see but a poor reflection.' He adds to this in his letter to the Philippians, where he writes:

> Not that I have already obtained all this ... I press on to take hold of that for which Christ Jesus took hold of me. I do not consider myself yet to have taken hold of it. But one thing I do: Forgetting what is behind and straining towards what is ahead, I press on towards the goal to win the prize for which God has called me heavenwards in Christ Jesus (Phil. 3:12-14).

This is his way of speaking not only for himself, but for all of us.

Paul, from his own experience, knew we see but a poor reflection as in a mirror. He had a quest for knowledge that would surpass any motivation of ours. He had had the best education that a person could have in those days, and possessed one of the greatest intellects in the history of the world. He wanted to know everything, but had to conclude that at best, we see but a poor reflection. So he knew it by experience. But he also knew it by revelation. God revealed to Paul that he could not know it all now, but that one day he would know: 'Whereas now I know in part, then I shall know fully, even as I am fully known.'

There are two main points that I want us to consider from this verse. The first is the limited possibilities of grace in this life, and the second, the unlimited possibilities of glorification in the age to come.

## The limited possibilities of grace now

The NIV translates this phrase as, 'We see but a poor reflection now as in a mirror,' whereas the KJV says, 'Now we see through a glass darkly.' There are two words in the Greek that are significant here. The first is best translated as 'mirror', because he is talking about what is reflected. The ancient world did not have mirrors like we have today, but Corinth was a step ahead of everybody else. Corinth was famous for producing some of the finest bronze mirrors in antiquity. Scholars have noticed that Paul only used this word twice in his writings, both times when addressing the Corinthians, because they would understand the word. He used it in this verse and he uses it in 2 Corinthians 3:18, 'We behold as in a mirror the glory of the Lord.'

The second word is 'darkly' (KJV), or 'poor reflection' (NIV). The Greek word is *einigmate* and this is the only time it is used in the Bible. From it we get our word, 'enigma'. An enigma is a puzzle, something that doesn't add up, because we can't understand it. Charles Wesley, in the hymn 'And can it be', wrote, ''Tis mystery all, the immortal dies, Who can explore his strange design?' You can't figure it out. The New English Bible translates this verse, 'Now we see only puzzling reflections in a mirror.' The Today's English Version translates it, 'What we see now is like the dim image in a mirror.' Paul's point is this: in this life there will be riddles that just won't be resolved. Any word of knowledge will give you only partial understanding. Any word of prophecy will give you only partial understanding. Any theological breakthrough will give you only partial understanding. Once in a while I get a breakthrough, and I think, 'Oh, I understand that verse! I've got it!' Then a week later, I think, 'Hang on, if that's true, then what about this?' All breakthroughs in this life lead to more questions. It is true in secular knowledge, the arts, the sciences. All knowledge is imperfect. It is an enigma. Why does God allow suffering? Does anybody know? Why did God create the possibility of sin? He didn't have to, did he? It is an enigma.

The apostle Paul is plainly saying that not all things are plain now. He is admitting that he doesn't understand it all. I often wish I had the apostle Paul with me to explain certain passages of the Bible, like Romans 7, or Ephesians 1:13 on the sealing of the Spirit. He could do it just like that. He could even tell us if he wrote Hebrews. Eventually, however, even after talking to the apostle Paul, we would have a question and he would just say, 'Well, you tell me.' Because now we know only indirectly, by reflection; now we know only in part. We get pieces of information, now and then, but at the end of the day, life is a riddle, an enigma. The possibilities of grace in this life are limited. But that is not the end of the story.

## The unlimited possibilities of glorification to come

'Now we see but a poor reflection as in a mirror; then we shall see face to face. Now I know in part, then I shall know fully, even as I am fully known.' When Paul uses the phrase, 'then face to face', he is referring back to Numbers 12:8, which reads, 'With him I speak face to face, clearly and not in riddles.' This partly explains 2 Corinthians 3:18, which sadly is only paraphrased in the NIV. The Greek reads, 'We see the glory of the Lord as in a mirror.' In 2 Corinthians 3 and 1 Corinthians 13:12 Paul is saying that all we can have of Jesus now is by reflection. Imagine being in church, but being unable to see the preacher directly, having instead to watch him in a strategically placed mirror. We are told that Jesus Christ, now that he has ascended into heaven and entered his glory, is so holy and awesome that no mortal could look straight at him and live. We couldn't do it, and so all we can have of Jesus here below, is by reflection. Peter, on the day of Pentecost, quoted David, 'I saw the Lord before me' (Ps. 16:8). But it was by reflection.

Or another illustration is the difference between seeing a photograph and then meeting the person face to face. This is similar to the point Paul is making. And in the case of Jesus, since his ascension into heaven, we see him only by reflection. That means we walk by faith, not sight. And even if we saw him in a vision, we wouldn't see him face to face, it would be by reflection. But one day that will change; John says, 'Dear friends, now we are children of God, and what we will be has not yet been made known. But we know that when he appears, we shall be like him, for we shall see him as he is' (1 John 3:2). We will be changed, and this is what is referred to as 'glorification'; we won't have sinful minds, or mortal bodies, rather we will be in a position to take in his glory, literally, face to face.

## When God tells us why

But Paul tells us something else will happen, too. Not only will we be changed and able look on the glorified Lord, face to face, but something wonderful will also happen – God will tell us why. God wants to tell us why, far more than we even want to know. But the patience of God is extraordinary. He can wait. He wants us to know the answers to our questions, but he can wait. We have to wait, but when we are glorified, God will tell us why. And Paul, to quote the Greek literally, says: 'Then I will know as even I am known.' By this he means known by God. Note, this is not a verse that *proves* that people will recognize each other in heaven. We *will* know each other in heaven, and we know that because on the Mount of Transfiguration, when Elijah and Moses appeared, Peter knew who they were. But that is not what this verse is saying. Rather, it is saying that I shall know, even as I am known by God. When you stop and think about it, what a promise it is: *I shall know*.

Perhaps this appeals only to the person who is agonized with questions, who really longs for God to explain something. Perhaps the question is, why is there a devil? Why didn't God just destroy the devil a long time ago? Why is there injustice? Why is there evil? But Paul says, 'One day I shall know.' F. F. Bruce has commented that the Greek word here, *epignosis*, should be translated as 'understand': one day I shall understand. God will make things plain.

Sometimes our questions are not on such a grand scale, but are more personal: Did I make the right decision? Lord, have I been living out of your will? Did I fail you? Have I fulfilled what you made me for?, and so on. Well, Paul says, 'Now we see but a poor reflection as in a mirror.' We see the Lord's glory only in a reflection, so we can't see things perfectly. The mirror that enables us to see ourselves has its limits: when we look at ourselves in a mirror we do so with a little bit of bias. We see we are getting older, but deny it is really true. James said, 'Anyone who listens to the word but does not do what it says is like a man who looks at his face in a mirror and, after looking at himself, goes away and immediately forgets what he looks like' (James 1:23-24). God's Word is the spiritual mirror by which we see our hearts, but even here our self-understanding is limited; we will always be prone to self-righteousness, and therefore, be unable to see ourselves as we really are. Sometimes I will say, 'Lord, show me.' But if I saw my wickedness directly, my mind would snap, I wouldn't be able to take it. If I saw the Lord's glory directly I would die. No-one can see God and live.

And so God graciously reveals things to us a bit at a time, like peeling the layers off an onion. With each new bit of understanding we might ask why we had to wait so long to get it right. But what Paul is saying is that, one day, when Gabriel blows his silver trumpet, it will be the loudest sound there ever was, carrying to the four corners of the earth. Some will be sleeping, some will be working, some will be sinning, some will be scoffing, some will be worshipping, but suddenly, a sound. The dead in Christ will hear it first. The souls under the altar who cried 'How long?' will hear that sound in their disembodied form, and then they will be transferred to their old bodies, except for one thing; they will be glorified bodies. The dust of the grave will be transferred into bodies like our Lord's when he was raised from the dead. And the dust of cremated bodies will do the same thing. We will be given perfect bodies, because Jesus 'will transform our lowly bodies so that they will be like his glorious body' (Phil. 3:21). In 1 Corinthians 15:51-55 Paul writes:

I tell you a mystery: We will not all sleep, but we will all be changed – in a flash, in the twinkling of an eye, at the last trumpet. For the trumpet will sound, the dead will be raised imperishable, and we will be changed. For the perishable must clothe itself with the imperishable, and the mortal with immortality. When the perishable has been clothed with the imperishable, and the mortal with immortality, then the saying that is written will come true: 'Death has been swallowed up in victory.'
'Where, O death, is your victory?
Where, O death, is your sting?'

We will be given perfect bodies. We will be given sinless minds. We will behold the Lord face to face and we will be changed. But now we see a poor reflection as in a mirror, but some day ...

> Some day he'll make it plain to me,
> Some day when I his face shall see,
> Some day from tears I shall be free,
> For some day I will understand.
> We'll talk it over in the by-and-by,
> I'll ask the reason –
> He'll tell me why.

# 18

# Why Not The Best?

'And now these three remain: faith, hope and love.
But the greatest of these is love'
1 Corinthians 13:13

Paul himself brings to an end this tremendous chapter. I wish Paul had said more about love, by which I mean I wish he had said more about how we can attain to this love. But he gave us what we have, and we are thankful for that.

1 Corinthians 13 is a parenthesis. By that I mean it is a kind of aside – an addition to a long discussion that began back in chapter 12, verse 1, when he said, 'Now about spiritual gifts, brothers, I do not want you to be ignorant.' Now Paul believes in all of the gifts, and he obviously has experienced every single one of them. But he was worried about these Corinthian Christians. They were sold on the gifts and, as we have seen, held them up as a sign of true spirituality, speaking in tongues, in particular. What Paul set out to show was, first of all, that not everybody has all of the gifts. He says so in chapter 12:30, 'Do all have the gifts of healing? Do all speak in tongues? Do all interpret?' But his main aim, however, is to show what we all *can* have. We cannot all interpret tongues, we cannot all prophesy, we cannot all speak in tongues, we cannot all do miracles, but we *can* all demonstrate the love of God, the 'most excellent way'. We may have not desired that love. It could be that if we had the choice, we would say, I would far prefer to speak in tongues,

or I would far prefer to have the gift of healing. But the apostle Paul, who has experienced them all, says the most excellent way is what he describes in 1 Corinthians 13.

Now we are going to look at this last verse, 1 Corinthians 13:13. Many scholars describe this as a triad, a set of three. Apparently, in the Christian church, even before the apostle Paul came along, this idea of the triad of faith, hope and love was common. Anyway, Paul often uses these three together. In Romans 5 he refers to a rejoicing in the hope of the glory of God. He started out by saying we are justified by faith, then he talks about rejoicing in hope, then he talks about the love of God shed in our hearts by the Holy Spirit. Again, in Galatians 5:5-6 we find this same set of three: 'By faith we eagerly await through the Spirit the righteousness for which we hope. For in Christ Jesus neither circumcision nor uncircumcision has any value. The only thing that counts is faith expressing itself through love.' This triad is also found in Colossians 1:4-5, 1 Thessalonians 1:3, and 5:8.

So Paul often brings these three together. But what is his reason for mentioning faith and hope in this passage on love? He hasn't been giving us a demonstration of faith, although he does mention faith briefly in verse 1, and he hasn't mentioned hope at all, so why did he bring them in? Verse 13:12 gives us a clue to the answer: 'Now we see but a poor reflection as in a mirror; then we shall see face to face. Now I know in part; then I shall know fully, even as I am fully known.' Faith and hope are important in connection with love, because, as we wait for the day when we shall see Christ face to face, we need to know how we should live. And what Paul does is to give three 'non-charismatic' possibilities: faith, hope, love. These three we live by as we await the day when all our questions will be answered.

First of all, let us look at the definitions of each of these words, and then compare them, before we go on.

## Defining faith, hope and love

### What is faith?

Faith is believing God. Many years ago, I was preparing to preach on faith, with Hebrews 11:1 as my text: 'Faith is the substance of things hoped for, the evidence of things not seen.' I thought there must be a better definition (Hebrews 11:1 is more of a description than a definition) and spent many hours of a journey discussing it with Dr. Lloyd Jones. But we did not come up with one. The next day, he telephoned me and said, 'Believing God – there's your definition.' And I knew then and I know now, one will not improve on that. So faith is believing God.

There are two kinds of faith: saving faith and achieving faith. Saving faith is how we become Christians; when we recognize that we have sinned against God, and that not even the best of our works will save us. The only way to be saved is to transfer the trust that we had in our good works to what Jesus did for us on the cross: 'While we were yet sinners, Christ died for us.' And when we trust Jesus Christ alone for our salvation, we are saved. That is saving faith.

But then there is achieving faith. It is this that we find described in Hebrews 11. Enoch, Noah, Abraham, Isaac, and so on, all of the great saints achieved things by faith. They were already saved, but they achieved things by faith.

When Paul refers to faith here he no doubt means both kinds. In Romans 5:1 he describes how, 'being justified by faith we have peace with God, through our Lord Jesus Christ', but in 1 Corinthians 13:12 he is also referring to the Christian life that is lived by faith. We live by faith, not by sight. So having just said, 'We now see but a poor reflection as in a mirror, then we will see face to face,' in the meantime, he goes on, 'these three remain,' and these three are possibilities for everybody. The first is faith; not all of our questions will be answered in this life, but we can live by faith.

### What is hope?

Hope is something to live for, or, to sum it up in one word it would be 'expectancy'. But I would add, expectancy even in suffering. Just as there are two kinds of faith, so also are there two kinds of hope. They are described as what is external to us, when something happens from outside to cheer us up, and also as that which is internal, when inside us the Holy Spirit does something that gives us hope. Either way, God can do it. Sometimes, we long for something to happen to cheer us up. Sometimes, many of us experience the feeling that we have got nothing to live for. But hope is having something to live for, and it can be something external to us that is given by God. It may be a friend, someone who promises something, giving us something to live for. It may be something practical, it may be something tangible, but somebody or something has happened that gives us hope; something to live for in the future.

But what about hope from the inside? 'God has poured out his love into our hearts by the Holy Spirit' (Rom. 5:5). God can give us a taste of himself. It is possible for God to speak so powerfully that right here, inside, we just know he has spoken. Often when I am preaching I long not only to speak the words of God, but to have the Holy Spirit come down on my listeners and have something happen in our hearts, something that just wells up and gives us something to live for because God has spoken powerfully to us.

What do we do when we have got questions but no answers, and we are not in heaven yet? Well, three things remain: faith, hope and love. So we come to love.

## What is love?

Love is brokenness. When God gets through to us, our stubborn will is broken and we become pliable, easy to manage. We are like soft putty in God's hands, and at long last God can use us. We have been broken. There are also two aspects to this love. We have seen two kinds of faith, two kinds of hope, now we will look at two kinds of love.

First, it is that which God graciously does for us, or I could say, in us. It is the pure love of God, when God himself comes in, takes over and enables us to face anything or anybody, enables us to forgive anybody for anything, and we can't believe it. When this happens we can feel like a spectator, and God is just doing it for us.

The second aspect of love is what *we* do, as a result of having been broken. It comes sometimes with effort, it is not easy. It is an act of the will, but we do it because it is right. Now it is not necessary for Paul to make this distinction between the two kinds of love because the other person would not know the difference between God doing it or us doing it because we have been broken. It is just that they can sense that we forgive them totally. We may be struggling – they don't know that, and we wouldn't want them to know that; if we did, then we haven't forgiven them totally. When we forgive totally, although we may be struggling inwardly, others won't have a clue. This is the result of being broken.

## Faith, hope, love – how they differ

There is an important difference to each of these. Firstly, faith has God, or the Word of God, as its object. It is almost impossible to tell the difference between God and his Word, when it comes to the object of faith. If I give you my word, you would be trusting my word, you would be trusting me. Do you see what I mean? And so, faith lives by the promise. We believe it, but we believe him.

So faith has the Word of God in mind. What about hope? Hope has the future in mind. It gives us something to live for and we are pulled along by the future. That's why we call it expectancy. What about love? Love mainly has others in mind. It is when we are broken and find ourselves living not for ourselves, but for Christ, who lived not to please himself but others. This is why with love there is no rival spirit, no desire to make another person envious, and no need to be vindicated because we know that God does that, and we aren't so sure that we deserve to be vindicated anyway. Love does that. When we are so convinced that we deserve to be vindicated, the chances are we have not been filled with the love of God. When we are filled with the love of God, we can see that there is so much about us that has been wrong, and God has not dealt with us as our sins deserve. There is so much that we have got away with. God has been so gracious. When we see this, how dare we want to see another person punished for what he did, when God hasn't punished us for what we did.

So faith has the Word in mind, hope has the future in mind, and love has others in mind. And Paul says that the greatest of these is love. But what if we are not too interested in loving others? If that is the case, we are exactly like the people in Corinth. They wanted certain gifts so that people would admire them, and Paul is trying to show them this is not the best way. There is a way that is not only better, but it is the best way, the most excellent way.

This is his last opportunity in this passage to make this point. I wish he had said more about how we may get this love, but he has told us what God wants us to know.

We have defined the three words in the triad, we have looked at their differences, and now I want us to consider their design.

### Faith, hope, love – what is their purpose?

The design of faith is to please God: 'Faith is being sure of what we hope for and certain of what we do not see' (Heb. 11:1). And faith pleases God: 'Without faith it is impossible to please God' (Heb. 11:6).

Whenever we trust God but the evidence for what we believe is lacking – God likes that. When we can say, 'Though he slay me, yet will I hope in him' – God likes that. If we can say with the three Hebrews: 'If we are thrown into the blazing furnace, the God we serve is able to save us ... but even if he does not ... we will not serve your gods' (Dan. 3:17-18) – God likes that. That is faith. It is believing God without the evidence. Other may call us fools, but this is where we stand. Faith is believing God, it is pleasing him.

What is the design of hope? Hope pleases us. Faith pleases God, hope pleases us. God does this for us because he knows we need it. He lets something happen to cheer us up, sometimes externally, sometimes internally. Either way, God does it. And so the design of hope is to please us by giving us something to live for, and God knows when to do that.

What is the design of love? It is to set others free. Faith pleases God, hope pleases us, love pleases others. We do for others what Jesus did because, essentially, it has to do with guilt. Most people have a problem with guilt, including most Christians. It may be the last thing we admit to, because often we feel guilty that we feel guilty. To be set free from guilt is the most wonderful thing in the world! The most wonderful thing we can do for another person is to set them free from guilt, because the most painful thing in the world is feeling guilty. There are some people that I don't want to be around because I know, in just seconds, I am going to get a heavy feeling. But the essence of love is keeping no record of wrongs, and the person who doesn't keep a record, who doesn't point the finger, is the person we want to be with. And that is the way Jesus is. People wanted to get next to him. He made them feel good. That's the essence of love. Faith pleases God, hope pleases us, love pleases others.

Faith, hope, love, are on ascending levels of power, each one a little higher than the previous one. It is not always easy to tell when faith is elevated to become hope, because there is a certain amount of overlap. But faith is developed by the Word and the Spirit, through preaching and by following the Spirit, and faith is further developed by going through a trial. And so, the link between faith and hope is trial. Faith leads to hope, which is preceded usually by considerable suffering, and hope is the reward for faith, the reward for dignifying the trial. God knows how much we can bear, and sooner or later, God steps in: '...after you have suffered a little while, [Christ] will himself restore you and make you strong' (1 Pet. 5:10). He steps in and restores us and makes us feel wonderful. Hope becomes ours, but the link between faith and hope is trial.

And hope leads to love. If trial is the link between faith and hope, the link between hope and love is character: 'We know that suffering produces perseverance; perseverance, character; and character, hope. And hope does not disappoint us, because God has poured out his love into our hearts by the Holy Spirit, whom he has given us' (Rom. 5:3-5). And so love is what hope leads to.

What is the dimension of each of these? What is the extent or the scope or the measure of each? Faith will give us the knowledge that we are pleasing God. There is nothing more wonderful than knowing we are pleasing God. I want to know that I am pleasing him. Well, faith pleases him.

Hope on the other hand pleases us. God does it, yes, but there is a sense in which it does little for the church at large. But love is where everybody benefits. Then there will be no rival spirit in a local church or between churches. So, at the end of the day, love, once it is experienced, will please us more than anything in the world. And that is because love is its own reward.

Now, we can be living by faith and living by love at the same time, because if we have love, then we have got the faith that we know pleases God. But with love we are set free not to think about ourselves all the time. We can be like Jesus to other people, and it is that which enables us to forgive others, to forgive ourselves, and to experience the pure love of God.

## The greatest of these is love

Why then, is the greatest of these three, love? There are two reasons. First, because with love everybody wins; what it does for others, what it does for everybody including ourselves. And second, because in terms of spiritual development or spiritual possibilities, love is as far as we can go. We don't go further than love, until we get to heaven. So if we want to know how holy we can be before we get to heaven, how godly, how much we can achieve at the spiritual level, it is not by having all the gifts of the Spirit. As far as we go is this, love – it is reaching the summit of Mount Everest, it is winning the gold medal, it is God's Nobel prize, it is the highest spiritual plateau to be reached this side of heaven. It is when we are self-effacing, truly meek, utterly willing to be behind the scenes. To use the language of 1 Corinthians 12, it is when you and I are willing to be the intestines, the gut, instead of the eye or the head of the body. Content to be behind the scenes, with nobody knowing what is happening, but it is what makes the body function. And there is no glory here below.

Love is the greatest, because this is true godliness. Some people think that godliness is just being strict, or severe – not dancing, not smoking, not drinking, not going to the cinema – but it doesn't take all that much of the Holy Spirit to come up with those things. Love, however, means never, never, never pointing the finger. It is the greatest, it is the best, it is when we become like Jesus. It is when we are so like him that sinners, instead of running from us when they see us coming, seek us out, when the rejects of society seek us out, when the alcoholics seek us out, when the addicts seek us out, when the poor seek us out. Because in us God is himself, the Spirit in us is ungrieved. We are at peace, no guilt at all. No guilt.

It is the best way to live, Paul says. I say, Why not the best for all of us?

# LETTING GOD LOVE US

**INTRODUCTION**

**A. A wrong understanding of the fear of God can result in the fear that God doesn't love us.**

**B. Whatever our theological background, most of us wrestle with the problem that God loves 'ME'.**
   1. *Those who lay stress on God's glory have the problem.*
   2. *Those who lay stress on God's tenderness have the problem.*
   3. *As a pastor I can safely state that it is often the hardest thing in the world for Christians to believe – 'that God really loves ME'.*
   4. *The question is, are we ready to let God love us?*

**C. What lies behind this difficulty in letting God love us?**
   1. *Some Christians have what is called an 'overly scrupulous conscience', a phrase that comes from Puritan studies.*
   2. *Some have a 'perfectionist' mentality.*
      (a) They are not content with trying, trying harder, doing your best, getting a 'pass', getting 90 per cent or even 99.9 per cent.
      (b) They feel they must produce 100 per cent in order to feel accepted; but nobody ever does.

---

This is an edited chapter from Dr. Kendall's book *Understanding Theology*, also published by Christian Focus. In addition to fitting in with the theme of *Just Love*, it shows the outline format that RT uses in *Understanding Theology* to explain important doctrines and practices of the Christian faith.

3. *It may be a psychological problem.*
   (a) Some cannot call God 'Father' and think it is a spiritual problem.
   (b) It is usually a mental block, something they cannot help, possibly because their only relationship with a father in this life was so poor.
4. *It may be due to a faulty theology.*
   (a) It may be because they have had a spiritual or theological diet with a one-sided emphasis on the fear, justice, wrath and/or sovereignty of God.
   (b) It may be because they are still living under the Old Covenant, under the Law, not unlike some Puritans.
      (i) Such virtually live under the promise of heaven, or assurance you are saved, by works of the Law.
      (ii) Such people often have little or no assurance of their own salvation, even if they have been professing Christians for years and years.
      (iii) Note:it is sadly true that many of the Puritans had no assurance of salvation even at the time of death.
5. *It may be because of personal failure, or sin.*
   (a) If we have let God down, especially if we've done it more than once, it is often difficult to believe God *still* loves us.
   (b) Rather than claim 1 John 1:9 – 'If we confess our sins, he is faithful and just and will forgive us our sins and purify us from all unrighteousness' – we often feel the need to 'perform' for him.
   (c) The result often is that we don't feel he loves us; if anything, we don't think he *should love us.*

## D. Why is this study important?
1. *Because our confidence and sense of well-being are at stake.*
2. *If we can each really and truly believe – and know – that 'God loves ME' we can face difficulties more easily – no doubt about it!*
3. *Our assurance of being saved is at stake.*
4. *The devil doesn't want us to believe that God loves us.*

5. *We are of more use to God in the world when we proceed under the conviction that we are truly and tenderly and everlastingly loved by God.*
6. *We please God most when we feel and affirm his love.*

## 1 ASSUMPTION: GOD LOVES US

A. **We begin with the general promise of John 3:16: 'For God so loved the world that he gave his one and only Son, that whoever believes in him shall not perish but have eternal life.'**

B. **What are the general promises?**
   1. *They refer not only to the world but to 'us'.*
      (a) 'But God demonstrates his own love for us in this: While we were still sinners, Christ died for us' (Rom. 5:8).
      (b) 'We love because he first loved us' (1 John 4:19).
      (c) 2 Peter 3:9: 'The Lord is not slow in keeping his promise, as some understand slowness. He is patient with you, not wanting anyone to perish, but everyone to come to repentance.'
   2. *Jesus died for everybody.*
      (a) 'For Christ's love compels us, because we are convinced that one died for all, and therefore all died. And he died for all, that those who live should no longer live for themselves but for him who died for them and was raised again' (2 Cor. 5:14-15).
      (b) 'But we see Jesus, who was made a little lower then the angels, now crowned with glory and honour because he suffered death, so that by the grace of God he might taste death for everyone' (Heb. 2:9).
      (c) 'My dear children, I write this to you so that you will not sin. But if anybody does sin, we have one who speaks to the Father in our defence – Jesus Christ, the Righteous One. He is the atoning sacrifice for our sins, and not only for ours but also for the sins of the whole world' (1 John 2:1-2).
   3. *The promise is to those who believe.*
      (a) 'This righteousness from God comes through faith in Jesus Christ to all who believe. There is no difference' (Rom. 3:22).

(b) 'He did it to demonstrate his justice at the present time, so as to be just and the one who justifies the man who has faith in Jesus' (Rom. 3:26).

(c) 'This is a trustworthy saying that deserves full acceptance (and for this we labour and strive), that we have put our hope in the living God, who is the Saviour of all men, and especially of those who believe' (1 Tim. 4:9-10).

**C. Once we meet the condition of faith in the general promises, the following absolutely apply to us:**
1. *We are loved with an 'everlasting love'* (Jer. 31:3).
2. *We are loved by Jesus himself* (John 13:34).
3. *We are loved by the Father with the same love that the Father loves Jesus himself (John 17:23).*

**D. Why should we let God love us?**
1. *Because he does.*
2. *Because he wants us to enjoy his love.*
3. *Because he chose us.*
    (a) *He chose us before we were born (Rom. 9:11; Eph. 1:4).*
    (b) *We love because he first loved us (1 John 4:19).*
4. *Because of God's grace.*
    (a) His grace and plan for us have *already taken into account our weaknesses:*
        (i)   Failure.
        (ii)  Unbelief.
        (iii) Self-righteousness.
        (iv) Fears.
    (b) The sacrifice of Calvary assures us that our sins are washed away.
        (i)   Jesus didn't die for us because he saw that we were going to turn out all right.
        (ii)  He died for us because he knew in advance we weren't going to come up to his standard.
        (iii) He died for us *because we were utterly unworthy.*
5. *Because he is God:* 'God is love' (1 John 4:16).
    (a) Only God can love like he loves.
    (b) There is no earthly frame of reference (parent, grand-

parent or close friend) who can match the way God really feels about his own.
(c) We desperately need the kind of love he has.

## 2 HOW WE LET GOD LOVE US
### A. Many of us won't let him love us.
1. *We are so used to rejection that we have a built-in defence mechanism that rejects him before he has a chance to show us how much he loves us.*
2. *I have watched people reject love the more you try to show it. Why?*
    (a) They are afraid it isn't really true.
    (b) They are afraid it won't last.
    (c) They basically mistrust any overture of love.

### B. What are the ways we block God's love?
1. *By trying to perform.*
    (a) This is what we do when we don't accept ourselves or believe his love toward us (1 John 4:16).
    (b) It is our way, consciously or unconsciously, of trying to get his approval by our good works.
2. *By refusing to feel good in his presence unless we are sure we have been 'making the grade'.*
    (a) This means we are going to feel pretty awful most of the time! (Jer. 17:9).
    (b) We need to be careful here, for when we feel 'good' in his presence in this manner we are vulnerable to self-righteousness – which he *doesn't* like!
3. *By not believing his love* (1 John 4:19).
    (a) In other words, it is sheer unbelief at work when we don't believe he loves us.
    (b) God says, as it were, 'Stop it!' But we often don't let that unbelief worry us – it should.
    (c) God is unhappy with us when we don't believe his own Word.
4. *By not believing we are forgiven even after we have confessed our sins:* 'If we confess our sins, he is faithful and just and will forgive us our sins and purify us from all unrighteousness' (1 John 1:9).

    (a)  This is a word to Christians.

    (b)  God goes to great lengths to show what it means if
we have truly confessed our sins; he is two things: (1)
Faithful – he will keep his Word. (2) Just – his justice
is intact when he forgives.

5. *By deliberate disobedience* (1 John 1:7).

    (a)  If we don't walk in the light we forfeit two things until
we re-commence walking in the light:

        (i)  Fellowship with the Father – intimacy.

        (ii)  The cleansing of Christ's blood – a good con-
science.

    (b)  When we deliberately disobey we cut off the lines of
communication whereby we feel his love.

        (i)  We are refusing to feel his love when we are in
disobedience.

        (ii)  We are not letting God pour out his love if we are
not sincerely wanting to please him.

## C. How do we feel his love?

1. *By confessing our sins once we realise we have sinned* (1
John 1:9).

    (a)  This means walking in the light (1 John 1:7).

    (b)  Walking in the light will reveal sin we hadn't been aware
of.

2. *By accepting ourselves.*

    (a)  Some say, 'I know God forgives me but I can't forgive
myself.'

    (b)  This is sheer self-righteousness.

        (i)  Are we wiser or better then God?

        (ii)  If we have confessed our sins we are obliged to
accept our forgiveness and accept ourselves.

    (c)  Not to accept ourselves is self-pity and unbelief, both
very displeasing to God.

3. *By quitting trying to 'perform'.*

    (a)  The greatest liberty is 'having nothing to prove'.

    (b)  When I believe that the blood of Jesus covers me, I will
enjoy that to the full!

    (c)  God paid the supreme price when he gave his Son to
die on the cross.

   (d) The most pleasing thing to God is to believe that his Son's blood cleanses us.

 4. *By disciplining ourselves to believe his love (1 John 4:16).*

   (a) At the beginning of the day I draw my own mind to two verses:

     (i) 'Let us then approach the throne of grace with confidence, so that we may receive mercy and find grace to help us in our time of need' (Hebrews 4:16).

     (ii) 'And so we know and rely on the love God has for us. God is love. Whoever lives in love lives in God, and God in him' (1 John 4:16).

 5. *By remembering that if our hearts condemn us,* 'God is greater than our hearts' (1 John 3:20).

   (a) God who is 'love' is *bigger than our faulty, deceptive hearts.*

   (b) *If I look at my heart I am going to feel awful most of the time!*

   (c) *God is big-hearted – magnanimous and gracious.*

     (i) 'For he knows how we are formed, he remembers that we are dust' (Psalm 103:14).

     (ii) He is not 'on the war-path' looking for every fault in us he can find.

     (iii) 'He does not treat us as our sins deserve or repay us according to our iniquities' (Psalm 103:10).

   (d) It doesn't take so much faith to believe God loves us when we are 'on top of the world'; but when we are at 'rock bottom' and affirm his love, God likes that very, very much.

## D. When should we affirm God's love?

 1. *When we are depressed.*

   (a) If we are able to affirm God's love when we are in this state it will be a great victory. It will show we really believe him!

   (b) Depression is largely overcome when we refuse to believe anything other than God's love for us.

 2. *When we have sinned.*

   (a) This is when we need God's love most.

   (b) Affirm his love by employing 1 John 1:9 – and believe it!

3. *When we are happy.*
   (a)  People often forget to be thankful when all is going well.
   (b)  Whereas people find it easier to weep with those who weep, only God can truly rejoice with those who rejoice (Rom. 12:15).

## E. How to accept God's love?
1. *Accept the friendship of people who will accept you.*
   (a)  Don't isolate yourself from people who want to be friendly.
   (b)  They may be 'angels without knowing it' (Heb. 13:2) whom God has put in your path.
   (c)  If you have been caught in a sin (Gal. 6:1), accept the person who challenges you with a meek spirit.
2. *Ask for more of the Holy Spirit* (Luke 11:13).
   (a)  The more you have of the Holy Spirit, the more you will feel God's love.
   (b)  Remember: the Spirit *is* God, who is love.
3. *Be loving in every way* (1 John 4:19).
   (a)  When we love (e.g., totally forgive those who have hurt us) we will feel loved by God.
   (b)  This is why John said, 'We love, because he first loved us.'
4. *Accept his disciplining with dignity* (Heb. 12:5).
   (a)  This is proof of God's love (Heb. 12:6ff.).
   (b)  It is proof of Jesus' own love! (Rev. 3:19).

## CONCLUSION
**God loves us as dearly as he loves his own Son, yet many of us have never fully accepted this fact.**

**We need to remind ourselves of those Scriptures that teach us of God's love and pray that by the Holy Spirit we will be able to allow ourselves to feel the wonder of the reality of God's love for us.**

**This love is not conditional: we do not need to be perfect. God loves us, no matter how unworthy we feel. Indeed I have known the greatest sense of God's love when I have felt the most unworthy and unlovable. This is the way Peter and the other disciples must have felt (John 13:37-14:1; 20:19).**

# Christian Focus Publications
## publishes books for all ages
Our mission statement –

*STAYING FAITHFUL*
In dependence upon God we seek to help make His infallible Word, the Bible, relevant. Our aim is to ensure that the Lord Jesus Christ is presented as the only hope to obtain forgiveness of sin, live a useful life and look forward to heaven with Him.

*REACHING OUT*
Christ's last command requires us to reach out to our world with His gospel. We seek to help fulfil that by publishing books that point people towards Jesus and help them develop a Christ-like maturity. We aim to equip all levels of readers for life, work, ministry and mission.

Books in our adult range are published in three imprints.
*Christian Focus* contains popular works including biographies, commentaries, basic doctrine and Christian living. Our children's books are also published in this imprint.
*Mentor* focuses on books written at a level suitable for Bible College and seminary students, pastors, and other serious readers. The imprint includes commentaries, doctrinal studies, examination of current issues and church history.
*Christian Heritage* contains classic writings from the past.

Christian Focus Publications, Ltd
Geanies House, Fearn,
Ross-shire, IV20 1TW, Scotland, United Kingdom
info@christianfocus.com

Can't find our books? You can buy them online:
www.christianfocus.com

# A Man After God's Own Heart

*God's Relationship with David and with You*

## R.T. Kendall

Twice God says that in King David he had found 'a man after my own heart' (1 Sam. 13:14, Acts 13:22). David was one of God's favourites. This was so despite David having sinned so deeply. What is encouraging is that the Lord continued to use David after his time of backsliding.

David was a man with deep feelings. He was a poet and musician as well as being Israel's greatest King and one of the greatest ever military leaders.

David wrote that 'the Lord confides in those who fear him' (Ps. 25:14). It is a great honour to have someone confide in you - but to think that God would confide in a human being is amazing! David was someone with whom God chose to share his heart.

If you wish to know what it is like to be confided in by God - to become a person after God's own heart too - then this book will help you discover what such a relationship is like.

ISBN 1-85792-382-0